CLASSIC VODKA

In the same series:

CLASSIC
VODKA

NICHOLAS FAITH &
IAN WISNIEWSKI

PRION

First published in Great Britain in 1997 by PRION BOOKS
32-34 Gordon House Road London NW5 1LP

Text copyright © Nicholas Faith & Ian Wisniewski
Design copyright © Prion
Editorial co-ordination by Lynn Bryan
Designed by Jill Plank

The authors hereby assert their moral rights
to be identified as authors of this work

A CIP catalogue record for this book is available from the British Library.
ISBN 1 85375 234 7

Printed in Hong Kong

CONTENTS

THE PURE SPIRIT

V ODKA IS ONE OF THE WORLD'S MOST UNDER-RATED DRINKS. UNFORTUNATELY FOR ITS REPUTATION, MOST DRINKERS TAKE IT FOR GRANTED. YET EXPLORING THE WORLD OF VODKA REVEALS A DRINK OF MANY FACETS.

Opposite
Moscow river in the
1840s when it was,
supposedly, the
source of pure water
for Moscow's
famous vodkas.

Vodka is a universal drink, and one that can be all things to all people. Nevertheless, despite its great variety, most drinkers use it merely as a neutral spirit, useful as a base for mixers, and valuable not only because of its lack of taste but also because it is a purer form of alcohol than its rivals. As a result it does not leave traces of alcohol on the breath, nor does it – up to a point anyway – induce a hangover. If this reductionist view enshrined the whole truth about vodka then it certainly would not be worth writing a book about so characterless a beverage. But even basic vodka, distilled to be

pure, does have its own identity, or, rather, as we shall see in this book, a number of identities. These derive from the raw materials employed, the ways it is distilled in different countries and the extremely wide variety of flavourings added to the liquid. Happily, and inevitably, the result is always a drink which provides an immediate sensation of warmth and comfort to the drinker.

But vodka is more, much more, than a neutral alcoholic base. It is, for one thing, deeply embedded in the mores, the hearts, and the souls of the people of Poland, Russia, Scandinavia and the Baltic states. They have each developed their own, infinitely more characterful vodkas, using very different raw materials – especially local water – to produce drinks which are subtle in themselves and subtly different from each other. They are not intended to be drunk with mixers, or as a speedy and inexpensive route to alcoholic oblivion but as an inherent part of social life; designed not to be gulped or hidden in a long drink, but to be sipped lovingly with the appropriate foods.

So although the neutral "international" vodkas are listed here, this book is primarily concerned with identifying the flavours, aromas, and characteristics found in those vodkas which are truest to the ideas of the people in whose countries they are distilled, and with describing how they should be drunk, especially in their historical context as the ideal accompaniment to so many of the traditional salty, spicy and preserved foods of Northern and Eastern Europe. Nevertheless, this book would not be complete without relating the extraordinary story of how a drink so closely associated with the frozen north, from Sweden to Siberia, became a global beverage. This expansion was a result of the diaspora of the Russian revolution, a saga which was to be echoed 40 years later when the Bacardi family left Fidel Castro's Cuba and transformed their family's ubiquitous spirit – white rum – into an international phenomenon.

But what is vodka? If you describe it, as you could, as a basically neutral spirit distilled from grain or potatoes, it could be categorized as merely one of the many other such drinks – like schnapps and aquavit – distilled from the same raw materials throughout Northern Europe for the past five centuries, to provide warmth and comfort during the long, icy winters. But whereas schnapps and aquavit (and gin for that matter) are made by taking a neutral spirit, immersing in it a wide variety of macerated herbs and flavourings and then redistilling the mixture, vodka is a pure spirit, the flavourings being added after the final distillation.

DISTILLATION

In theory distillation is the simplest of industrial processes, based on the fact that alcohol boils at a lower temperature than water. So, in theory, nothing could be simpler than to boil a suitable raw material in an enclosed container, draw off the alcoholic fumes at the top and then cool or condense them. This historic procedure remains the principle behind the "pot-still" method – distillation in a pot – used for most of the world's finest spirits, including cognac, malt whisky, and a handful of vodkas. But most spirits, including a majority of even the very best vodkas, are made in "continuous stills". As the name implies these produce spirit continuously, not in batches. Because, by definition, a continuous still operates continuously, and there is no need to heat up each batch of raw material separately, it is much more efficient than the pot-still. The continuous still was invented in the first half of the 19th century and only spread gradually to

countries that produced vodka, so that every drop made before 1830, and most of what was distilled in the latter half of the 19th century, was made in pot-stills.

Obviously there are an enormous number of variables in the types of spirit produced in the world. The variety can be caused by the method of distillation, the nature of the raw materials, which provide the finished product with its character, and the strength of the product, which depends not only on the type of still employed but also on the strength of the spirit.

A spirit distilled until it is pure 100 per cent alcohol will not have any impurities, and thus no discernible taste. But in a spirit distilled to 96 per cent, the norm with many continuous stills, you will begin to discern the aromas and flavours of the raw materials. The spirit's character becomes ever-more defined as the alcoholic strength decreases and it has a higher level of impurities, so that an armagnac distilled to a mere 55 per cent is full of impurities, only some of which will be palatable.

Throughout its history – and never more so than today – vodka has been the object of an underlying tension between those looking for purity at any cost and those looking for positive qualities. The contrast between the two can be dramatic: a commercially-produced vodka where the emphasis is on purity and neutrality alone may have only 30 milligrams of flavouring matter for every litre of spirit, whereas the figure for whiskies and cognacs can be up to 2,500 per litre.

FERMENTATION

The term "raw material" for what goes in to the still is misleading, since the still can only process a product which is already alcoholic. This involves taking some form of vegetable matter and relying on the enzymes in yeasts to convert sugar – whether in sugar cane, wine or beer – into alcohol. In the case of vodka the convenient raw material to use is molasses, the

Opposite
The incidence of high-strength spirits in Poland and Russia originally had a lot to do with the severe winters, when only strong liquors could be transported by traders; lower-proof alcohols invariably froze.

11

Opposite
An old Swedish
distillery with a
pot-still on
the right.

major by-product of sugar refining which is already full of sugar. But it is also the least satisfactory of all of the various types of raw materials because it provides only sweetness without any more positive qualities. Beetroot used to be widely utilized to make cheap vodka but two other types of raw materials, grain and potatoes, are full of potentially valuable flavours and form the basis of all the finest vodkas. Potatoes are the most demanding raw material of all since some form of grain is needed to convert their starch into fermentable sugar.

Whether the distilling process uses pure grain or potatoes-plus-grain, the raw material is steeped in shallow open vats and is then allowed to germinate into malt. Yeasts are added and these convert the malt into a type of beer or "wash", which generally measures about eight per cent alcohol by volume (abv), less than a tenth of the final product which finally emerges from the still, and the same as the basic wine used to make cognac.

DISTILLATION

The pot-still remains the simple affair it has
been since the Dutch perfected its design in the
16th century. It is circular, made of copper
(which helps to remove many of the
impurities), and the fumes are led from the top
to a separate cooler or condenser. For centuries
before this, vodka was usually made in much
less satisfactory containers – pots rather than

Above left
Typical wooden
storage vats which
could contaminate
the vodka if they
were dirty.
Above right
Modern stainless
steel vats at the
Bielsko-Biala
distillery in Poland.

specially designed stills. This meant that the alcohol was full of "fusel oils", a term which covers a multitude of undesirable evil-smelling compounds. These could be eliminated by subsequent redistilling to "rectify" (purify) the spirit, a process which removed all the qualities, good or ill. Alternatively, the taste could be disguised – hence the tradition of additives such as herbs, spices, fruits and honey – or the spirit could be filtered.

In the late 18th century it was discovered that charcoal not only removed many impurities from the spirit, but also added its own warmth and smokiness. This has ensured its status as a principal element in many famous vodkas. The Russians maintain that this crucial improvement in purification techniques was the result of research by the chemist Theodore Lowitz, commissioned by the Tsar in 1780. Credit has also been claimed, however, by the Smirnoff family in Russia, as well as by the Swedes and the Poles.

The continuous still, which costs far more to build but far less to operate than the pot-still, was first introduced in the 1830s. Although it is generally associated with the name of Aeneas Coffey, an Irish customs official, it seems to have been one of the many inventions which were developed simultaneously in a number of countries. The heart of the continuous still is a cylindrical column containing a number of plates jutting out across the interior. Steam is introduced at the top, the wash at the bottom and they bounce back and forth across the plates in a process which separates out the alcoholic vapours. These are then captured and cooled in a condenser. In contrast to the pot-still method, the strength of the final spirit can be controlled: the more plates the still contains the more opportunity the spirit will have to distil and the stronger the result. While it is tempting to assume that pot-still production is inherently superior, if only because it is the more traditional, more romantic system, the distillers themselves will say that both methods produce similar results, even for the finest vodkas.

The techniques used by modern distillers rely heavily on the purity of the final spirit, using more than one distillation column to achieve the desired result. This does not mean that all vodkas are the result of technical sophistication – quite a few of those made in Russia or Western Europe are the result of low-strength

distillation which has left traces (or even greater proportions) of impurities.

Ultimately the differences between vodkas arise from three factors: first, and crucially, the raw material used (see below); second the water – particularly noticeable in the quality of Sibirskaya and Finlandia; and third, the methods and techniques used for filtration – each major distiller claims to have a secret and inevitably superior method. But the ability of modern distillation techniques to remove impurities in a single, double (in the case of Smirnoff) or triple (in the case of Absolut) rectification process means that character is now often provided after distillation by adding a comparatively less rectified spirit. For instance Absolut adds a trace of a separately distilled lower-strength spirit to preserve some of the more desirable impurities, or "congeners" as they are known.

Opposite
At some distilleries, such as Bielsko-Biala, the vats are veritable historic monuments.

THE RAW MATERIALS

Vodka can be produced from a wide variety of raw materials: millet, barley, rye, maize, wheat, beetroot, onion, carrot, apple, pumpkin, bread, chocolate and even whey, the essential criterion being a starch content that can be converted to sugar. With so many possible raw materials there is no standard recipe for vodka, but not all of them are used on a commercial scale and the most common are grain, particularly wheat and rye, as well as potatoes and molasses.

Whatever the raw material, the key issue for distillers is removing the impurities which all spirits initially contain, and, depending on the style of the vodka, retaining the positive characteristics of the raw material. The first distillation, which can be up to 80 per cent abv removes the majority of impurities (the higher the percentage of protein in a raw material, the higher the level of fusel oils, which the distiller

must remove). The second distillation (up to 96.4 per cent abv) deals with the remaining impurities, but also reduces the character of the raw material in the process. The secret lies in balancing purity with character.

While the quality of neutral spirit depends on the skill of the distiller as much as the raw material, even among spirits at 96.4 per cent abv there is a perceptible hierarchy according to the raw material used. Grain is ranked first, and molasses usually last, the difference being evident to an expert nose even at 96.4 per cent, and of course more readily apparent on the palate when the spirit is diluted to bottling strength. However, over the last 10 years in

particular, there has been such significant progress in distilling technology, that the quality margin between different raw materials is beginning to narrow, although molasses still cannot compete with grain or potato in terms of character.

Opposite
Waving fields of
Polish rye, ripening
for the distiller.

Ultimately, the choice of raw material has to take into account the quality of the end result, as well as cost and tradition. It is usually a case of harvesting the local source of starch, which explains both Scandinavia and Russia's use of wheat, while Polish vodka capitalizes on rye and potatoes.

Potatoes usually give a sweeter aroma and flavour than grain, though rye also yields a natural, subtle sweetness. Connoisseurs now rank potato vodka alongside that made from grain. However, potato vodka is still subject to a certain snobbery, as though it is a consolation spirit made in the bath-tub. This misconception can be traced back to a time when potatoes were the cheapest raw material for vodka, whereas today, they are generally more expensive and labour-intensive than grain. They must be cleaned and steamed to "liberate" their starch and be liquefied. They are then pressed into mash vats and malted. The resulting "sweet mash" is fermented to provide a strength of about 7–11 per cent abv, before being distilled and rectified, transforming what is initially an aggressive smell into a more fragrant asset.

Polish potato vodka is produced from industrial potatoes, which have a minimum starch content of 18 per cent, though usually around 20-22 per cent. (Standard potato varieties have only a 10-12 per cent starch content.) High-starch potatoes are cultivated in specific areas with ideal microclimates, along the Baltic coast and along the banks of the River Vistula.

Other technical differences between potatoes and grain are also significant to the distiller. The higher level of pectin in potatoes, which is responsible for producing methanol, means that they contain about 10 times more methanol than grain. Another consideration is that the by-products of potato vodka are more complex and expensive to dispose of than those of grain. Furthermore, the yield compares poorly: 100kg of potatoes yield about nine litres of spirit, while the same amount of grain produces around 25-32 litres.

Wheat–based vodka is made from soft (as opposed to hard) wheat. Hard wheat contains a higher level of gluten (which the distiller has to remove), and is used, for instance, in breadmaking. Winter wheat is used by distillers in preference to spring wheat. Planted in the autumn and not harvested until the following August/September, winter wheat is about six months older than spring wheat, and offers a correspondingly higher level of starch.

Some distilleries choose not to strip bran from the grain, but this is a false economy as bran produces methanol which must be removed at a later stage. During wheat vodka production gluten is coagulated in the initial "cooking" process, and can be sold as a by–product, which helps to make it a more economical raw material. Wheat also has a lower level of congeners to contend with than rye (untreated congeners create "off" flavours and cause hangovers).

While prices vary from country to country, wheat can be less expensive than maize. However, maize has a higher starch content which means that it yields a higher level of spirit than wheat. Maize is also considered to produce a spirit that is similar in quality to wheat, particularly when the aim is neutrality.

While there are clear differences between vodkas made from various raw materials, there are of course distinctions to be drawn between vodkas made from the same raw material. In addition to distillers imposing their own individual styles, different varieties of wheat, for instance, result in different styles of vodka. A vital influence on the eventual flavour of

vodka is water, though it is not generally considered a raw material. Poland's Polmos distilleries all use the same recipe for classic vodka brands, yet distillers say there is a discernible difference between bottles of the same brand produced in each of the 25 separate distilling locations, reflecting their respective water source. The exceptional qualities of the finest Finnish and Russian vodkas are also attributable to the quality of the water.

Meanwhile technical advances continue, enabling distillers to produce better quality spirit from a wider range of raw materials. But even so, the traditional raw material hierarchy is not going to be challenged.

FLAVOURED VODKAS

While clear vodka is now the predominant style, vodka was originally flavoured with herbs, reflecting its medicinal rather than social status. Moreover, as early distillers were unable to rectify spirit, and so remove the impurities which created unpleasant flavours and aromas, they tried instead to conceal them by adding aromatic ingredients and by using honey as a sweetener. In this way, what began as a series of practical measures helped to develop a speciality vodka genre.

Flavoured vodka is now increasingly making its mark, though the range available is not as extensive as it was in the 18th and 19th centuries when there were over a hundred varieties on the market.

Intense competition in today's vodka market has put the onus on distillers to develop their range of flavours, in order to gain new customers and increase market share. That naturally raises the question of what is an authentic flavouring, as opposed to a commercial "gimmick".

The usual criteria for authenticity are tradition and the use of indigenous ingredients. That being the case the highest pedigree would be awarded to a Polish vodka such as Zubrowka, which dates from around the 16th century. Zubrowka is flavoured with bison grass from the Bialowieza Forest in eastern Poland. This wild grass is picked while in full bloom during the summer, the theory being that the higher the temperature, the better the eventual flavour. Techniques of drying and harvesting the grass, as well as distilling methods, create a highly aromatic, herbaceous vodka.

Meanwhile, Okhotnichaya (Russian Hunter's vodka) contains port, orange and lemon zest, ginger, cloves, coffee, peppers, juniper and anise. While this line-up includes some imported ingredients, no one would question its authenticity.

Similarly, pineapple vodka was recently launched by both Finlandia and Wyborowa. While this is not an indigenous flavouring, pineapple does have a certain tradition, already having been cultivated in glasshouses in 19th-century Poland.

When judging a flavoured vodka, the ultimate criterion should be, simply, whether or not the flavour is a success on the palate. And of course, flavours like pineapple are being launched in response to consumer demand.

Rectified spirit is generally used as a basis for flavoured styles, and grain such as wheat and rye effectively underline a range of ingredients, though potato spirit is also used.

Poland and Russia boast the widest range of flavoured vodkas, spanning such ingredients as rowan berries, juniper, honey, pepper, lemon, blackcurrant and cherries. While some styles

are produced by both countries, there are significant differences in the ingredients used. Russian lemon vodka, Limonnaya, for example, uses lemon peel, while the Polish version, Cytrynowka uses lemon tree leaves as well as lemon peel. Similarly, both countries produce Starka, an aged vodka. The Poles blend unrectified rye spirit with a tiny amount of Malaga wine, which is aged for a minimum of 10 years in small oak casks. The Russians combine grain spirits flavoured with an infusion of apple and pear tree leaves, together with brandy and port.

The vodka with the largest number of flavourings is claimed by Poland, with Gnesnania Boonekamp, a bitter vodka, containing 23 herbs and spices. Gold leaf is one

Above
An old Polish grocer's shop dominated by a display of Lancut vodka bottles.

Opposite
Honey liqueur – an old Polish tradition.

Opposite
Bottles of the classic bison-grass vodka.
Below
The herbal tradition continues.

of the most unusual flavourings, which the Poles use to make Goldwasser.

Flavouring spirit can be a very simple process – blending ingredients such as aromatic oils, rather like mixing a very long drink. However, the more traditional approach to flavouring is maceration. While many distillers are secretive about the processes they use to flavour vodka, the Poles are unusually forthcoming. In Poland flavourings such as fruit and herbs are generally prepared in two ways, using either the classic maceration or the circulation method.

In the classic method the ingredients are macerated in spirit which varies in strength (usually 40-60 per cent abv) according to the type and ripeness of the ingredients. After the first four weeks the spirit is drained (and reserved), with another batch of spirit added for a further three-week maceration. These two liquids are blended, together with a residual liquid pressed from the macerated ingredients. All three "spirits" are then adjusted to a standard alcoholic strength, prior to bottling.

Polmos
STRONG VODKA
HERBS
ziołowa mocna

44% alc./vol.   0,75 l

PRODUCE OF POLAND
BIELSKO-BIAŁA

The circulation method uses ingredients such as bison grass, spread across a sieve inside a steel tank. Alcohol circulating in the tank passes through the sieve twice every eight hours, over a period of four to seven days, again according to the ripeness and type of ingredients. The circulation method is faster, considered more economical, and increasingly preferred.

In both methods the flavoured spirit is pumped into barrels where it settles and the flavours fuse. This lasts a minimum of two weeks, and often up to several months, depending on the flavourings. Old barrels are used so that the wood has minimal impact on the flavour, with the same barrels obviously used for the same flavourings. Barrels yield a much better result than steel tanks for "resting" flavoured spirit. During the resting period, evaporation results in the spirit decreasing in strength by around nine per cent abv, which is adjusted prior to bottling.

Another ingredient used in Poland for preparing flavoured vodka is mors. This is freshly pressed fruit juice combined with rectified spirit, resulting in a strength of 16-20 per cent abv.

Once all the ingredients have been prepared, blending is a fully automated, computerized process, with some flavoured vodkas containing up to 15 or more different elements.

While flavoured vodka traditionally reflects the colours of its ingredients, current consumer

preference is for clear vodka, which has resulted in "clear flavoured vodka" being produced by various countries. Colourless aromatic oils, such as lemon, can simply be added to rectified spirit and usually bottled without a resting period. Another approach used by various distillers to produce clear flavoured vodka, is macerating ingredients such as fruit zest in vodka and distilling the resulting liquid. This "flavoured distillate" is then blended with vodka at the same stage as adding water (which reduces the spirit to bottling strength).

Whether flavoured vodkas regain their former popularity and variety remains to be seen. Meanwhile, traditional as well as innovative flavours are being promoted by more and more companies.

CHAPTER ONE

THE HISTORY OF VODKA

VODKA IS DEEPLY IMBEDDED IN THE
CONSCIOUSNESS OF A WHOLE REGION.
IT IS AN IMPORTANT ELEMENT IN THE
ECONOMIC, SOCIAL AND CULTURAL LIFE
OF MANY NORTHERN EUROPEAN COUNTRIES.

Opposite
A Moscow street in the late 18th century complete with bar – and police station.

Over the past thousand years three countries – Sweden, Poland and Russia – have dominated the Northern European region. For all three peoples – as well as their former subjects in Finland, the Baltic states and the Ukraine – vodka is much more than a drink. It is a way of life. Consequently, nothing is more fascinating than to trace the very different relationships between these Northern European peoples and their beloved drink, vodka, throughout history. Nevertheless, they all have a number of factors in common: a long

history, and a love-hate attitude. Love because
the drink is invariably the essence of
friendship, of gregariousness – and because
vodka is such an ideal accompaniment to so
many of the region's salted and preserved
foods; hate because use so often leads to abuse,
to a state of alcoholic despair.

RUSSIA

Russia's claim that vodka was first distilled on Russian soil is rightly disputed. It is, however, safe to say that in no other country does vodka form so essential a part of cultural life, nor is any other country's identity so bound up with the drink, for good or ill. Stephen White quotes some classic Russian sayings: "Without vodka friendship is no longer friendship, happiness is no longer happiness."

"It warms people in the cold, cools them in the summer heat, protects them from the damp, consoles them in grief and cheers them when times are good."* Even William Pokhlebkin, the staunchest defender of Russian vodka, has to admit that it has two faces, as "the elixir sipped sociably and as the comforter, the deadener of pain, the anaesthetic without which life would be unendurable".**

But throughout modern Russian history there has always been a drink problem associated almost exclusively with vodka, and even more importantly, with the way it was drunk. It wasn't that the Russians drank, or drink, more than people of other nationalities, but that they concentrated on drinking vodka in excessive bouts.

* *Russia Goes Dry*, Cambridge University Press, 1996
** *A History of Vodka*, Verso, London, 1992

Not surprisingly vodka has traditionally played a central role in Russian public policy. Russian rulers have always needed the revenue from vodka, which at times amounted to two-fifths of the national total – but they also needed a sober population, and, more particularly, sober armed forces. Clearly, this meant a delicate balance of interests.

Historically, vodka, the drink, was being distilled well before the word came into general use. The name is the diminutive of *voda*, meaning water, emphasizing the central place it occupies in Russian life. For a long time vodka was described by many other names, especially *vino*, wine. It could be called *perevara*, signifying that it was made from mead and beer, or as *korchma* – hooch or pot wine. Indeed the term vodka was used to describe a medicinal potion rather than a social beverage.

Vodka is the aunt of wine.
— **OLD RUSSIAN SAYING**

The Russians obviously decided early on that their national drink was something special, unrelated to any spirit produced by other countries. The word vodka is important because it marks a linguistic, and thus a cultural distinction from the many other words (the Scandinavian *aquavit*, the Gaelic *uisge beatha*, the French *eau de vie*) derived from the original

33

Latin name for a distilled spirit, *aqua vitae*, the water of life. Moreover the Russians never used the term "burnt" which is employed in most other languages, from the German *branntwein* (burnt wine) to the Anglo-Saxon brandy, and the derivatives in Ukrainian of *goreloe* or *goriaschchee*, again implying a burnt liquid.

In order to produce vodka a plentiful supply of grain, preferably rye, is needed, and this became possible in the 12th century, once what we now call Russia had emerged as a state based on the northern Volga round Moscow. The new country was cut off from the influence of the Byzantine Empire based in Constantinople, and soon developed its own fermented liquors, beer, ale, and above all mead and *kvas*, the beer-like liquid made from a variety of grains, often flavoured with herbs and spices. But to use these fermented brews as a base for a drinkable spirit required another technical revolution.

This may have happened as a by-product of one of the country's basic industries, the extraction of pitch from pine logs by boiling them in water in pits. It was only one step further to boil a fermented brew in a closed pipe and then capture the alcoholic vapours as they emerged, and for some time the same term was used for the production of both pitch and alcohol. Unfortunately this method ensured that the ethyl alcohol, containing the elements of what we now think of as potable spirits, boiled off, while the liquid that remained in the pipe or pot contained the heavier congeners, the foul-smelling elements known as fusel oils. The only solution to the problem was either to disguise them with aromatic herbs and spices, or keep redistilling until some of them had been removed, although this involved losing all the positive characteristics of the spirit as well. It was precisely this problem which led to the idea of vodka as a neutral spirit, one that could be flavoured with almost any local ingredient (see page 23).

Distilling techniques became less crude in the second quarter of the 15th century when Russian rulers absorbed lessons on distilling techniques from foreign knights and merchants – a Genoese delegation demonstrated distilling techniques to the Grand Duke of Lithuania in 1426 and in the 1430s a delegation from the Russian church visited Italy, a journey which provided the clergy with an opportunity to study the distillation techniques being employed in some of the country's monasteries. At the same time the Russians started the "three-field system" of crop rotation which multiplied grain production within a few years, thus providing the necessary surplus for vodka production. Technical advances also reduced dependency on honey, the base of mead, as the primary source of alcoholic liquor. From the 15th century on, indeed, liquid measurements were standardized in line with that used to measure vodka – the bucket.

In 1478 the Tsar introduced a general policy of protectionism and it was at this point that his government started to take an interest in vodka's revenue potential. By 1533 the first "Tsar's tavern" or *kabak* had been opened in Moscow and trade in the spirit was exclusively reserved for the state. Over the centuries vodka became an ideal source of revenue, whether directly, through state monopolies, or indirectly, its production and sale privatized by being farmed out to local capitalists, the notorious tax farmers, in return for regular and substantial payments to the government. By 1648 there were even tavern revolts as a result of the system, which included spirit that had been adulterated or made from inferior raw materials like potatoes and beets – and the inability of the urban poor to pay the debts they had run up at the Tsar's taverns. The vodka sold by the tax farmers was no better. Stephen White quotes a report showing that their vodka was "horribly adulterated" with herbs being used to flavour spirit which had been diluted.

Opposite

Moscow 1816 – where, for the aristocracy, vodka drinking had become a proud statement of national identity.

For three centuries after distillation techniques were first established, the finest vodka was made exclusively from rye and until the 1917 revolution rye continued to account for over half of total vodka production, the balance being made from wheat and potatoes. Even when other raw materials were used for the fermentation process, rye malt remained an essential ingredient, together with small but

crucial quantities of barley, buckwheat, oat flakes, wheat bran and cracked wheat. Originally these additional elements were merely the detritus from a nobleman's mill, but eventually they were recognized as conferring additional qualities to the mix.

The Russian aristocracy usually followed the French lead in gastronomy as representing the acme of civilized life. By contrast the production and appreciation of fine vodkas was a statement of their independent national identity. In this they were following Tsar Peter the Great, who loved his vodka triple-distilled, diluted with anis water and then redistilled, and was most unhappy when he was reduced to drinking cognac and other lesser foreign spirits on his travels to Western Europe. Being technically minded he also contributed designs for an improved pot-still.

Before Peter came to the throne in the late 17th century most Russians used honey to dilute and improve the flavour of their vodkas. By the late 19th century it had become less necessary to disguise the original taste of vodka, but improvements in distillation techniques were still needed to refine an inevitably disagreeable spirit. Distillers used coagulants like bread, egg whites – also used in refining expensive wines – ashes, potash and soda, to remove the grosser impurities, until the discovery in the course of the 18th century that charcoal provided an incomparable method of filtration. Although some aristocratic distillers could afford to use alder charcoal, most compromised on the less absorbent but widely available charcoal made from Russia's immense birch forests. The spirit had to be diluted before it was filtered, because charcoal could not remove the oily contaminants from strong spirit. As time went on the filtration qualities of the charcoal were steadily improved by preparing the wood properly and removing its bark and any knots.

By then the Russians were beginning to use not only anis but also herbs and spices, collectively known as *zel'e*. Most of these were native additives. Pokhlebkin lists "forest herbs, the young buds of various Russian trees (birches, willows and pussy-willows), leaves

(cherry and blackcurrant) and foreign spices, amaranthus cloves etc" – a range which expanded greatly in the first half of the 19th century. But gradually, and generally only with "aristocratic" vodkas, the additives were employed less to disguise unpleasant aromas than to enhance the basic product, resulting in a variety of aromatic vodkas, many of which – like pepper vodka – are unequalled in flavour.

By the end of the 19th century, thanks to the influence of the great chemist D I Mendeleyev,

 CLASSIC VODKA

who had a considerable interest in vodka production, an ideal vodka had been defined. As Pokhlebkin puts it, "Russian vodka – or more precisely, Moscow vodka – came to be considered as a product consisting of grain spirit, triple-distilled and then diluted with water to a concentration of 40 per cent" – today's standard, but stronger than had previously been produced. Pokhlebkin rightly based his claim that Moscow-distilled vodka was superior on the softness of the city's water supply, which came from the Moscow and Neva rivers (and, above all from the Mytishchi springs 20 kilometres from Moscow) – and in the 1920s when water was brought in from other sources the quality of the vodka did indeed decline.

The distillation process remained true to the old rules which demanded that it be as slow as possible and that less than half the volume of wort (fermented broth) be distilled off. Landowners did not mind that the final yield of spirit was a mere two per cent of the original volume of mash of yeast and malt, for the grain came free from their peasants, who worked for virtually nothing, while the wood came from their own forests.

But these vodkas were the exception, and the last Tsars had to reintroduce a state monopoly at the end of the 19th century, partly to stop the consumption of lesser, poisonous spirits produced by non-noble distillers.

Opposite
Siberian birch trees are one of the best raw materials for the charcoal used in vodka filtration.

Opposite

A rather idealized family and friends picnic outside a Russian dacha.

One of the first effects of the 1917 revolution was that vodka was banned by the new regime, as a symbol of its desire to replace bad old habits with those more in keeping with a Brave New World. For there had been a frightening degree of drunkenness associated with the first great triumph of the revolution, the assault on the Winter Palace in the city of Saint Petersburg in October 1917. Wave after wave of revolutionary soldiery collapsed, drunk, and order was only restored by the Finnish regiment, led, according to American journalist John Reed "by men with anarcho-syndicalist leanings, [who] declared a state of siege and announced that they would blow up the wine cellars and shoot plunderers on sight".

Until 1936, or so the official history makes out, only beer, wine and vodka up to a strength of 20 per cent abv could be sold, controlled by a very profitable national monopoly. Then came the deluge: Stalin and his satellites found that vodka was a useful weapon to deaden the sensibilities of his terrified subjects during the Great Terror, and throughout the war vodka was issued as part of the troops' regular rations, a step perhaps justifiable in wartime but a guarantee that the country would face a massive alcoholism problem once the war was over.

For the next 40 years Stalin and his successors continued to pursue this policy. The price of vodka was kept low, and an official silence was maintained over the endemic alcoholism that

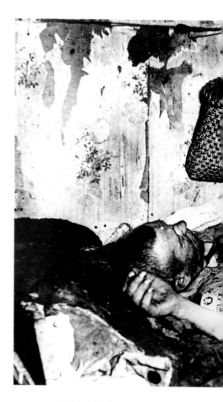

Right
Serious drinking in a Moscow cellar in pre-Revolutionary Russia. Vodka as a symbol of Russian identity has always had its dark side of rampant alcoholism and nihilistic solace.

infected every aspect of life in the Soviet Union. Vodka relieved the stress of daily existence. It gave some temporary warmth and comfort to workers in hostels, on building sites in icy temperatures, to the lonely, and the embittered – in other words to the majority of the Russian people. Even more dangerous was the endemic alcoholism in the armed forces – the MIG 25, Russia's most advanced fighter, became known

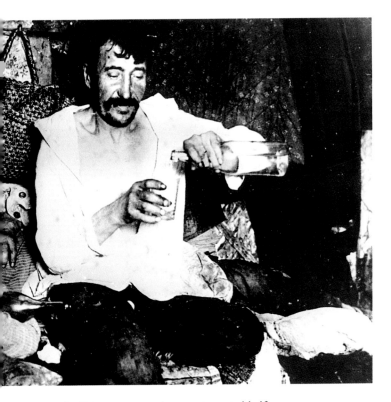

as the flying restaurant because it carried half a ton of (drinkable) alcohol in its braking systems. As Pokhlebkin says, by the 1970s "drunkenness on the job became the norm, an everyday occurrence". Vodka, consumed in alarming quantities by leaders such as Leonid Breshnev and Konstantin Chernenko, who died from cirrhosis of the liver, became the preponderant cause of suicides and accidents

on the roads, in the home and in factories. Drying-out clinics were established for overly aggressive drunks, but that was all.

Gorbachev cited the country's alcohol problem as a symbol of its decline, albeit partly because his brother-in-law was an alcoholic. He increased prices and imposed a series of theoretically strict limits on vodka production and on its consumption in public. But his policy was applied in an old-style Communist fashion – imposed from the top down – and did not attack the roots of the problem, which were the country's social and economic conditions. The authorities merely drove national alcoholism underground which resulted in an enormous growth in the distillation of *samogon*, the dangerous illicit brew which had been the mainstay of the Russian drinking classes during previous periods of austerity.

Oddly, the upheavals since 1985 do not seem to have affected this particular staple of Russian civilization. Moscow still rules, still sets the technical standards, so much so that only vodkas distilled in Moscow, or under the supervision of the technicians it employs, is reckoned to be of superior quality. The export set-up is also relatively unchanged. Sojuzplodoimport (SPI) is a monopoly, acting through a joint venture, Plodimex, based in Hamburg. It was established in 1974 as a barter organization, selling vodka, one of the few Russian exports of any quality, in return for much-needed Western goods. The only significant exception is a joint venture between SPI and Grand Metropolitan, the parent company of IDV (International Distillers & Vintners), owners of Smirnoff. The 1995 agreement aims to promote Stolichnaya as a world brand. IDV is hoping to use "Stolly" in its brand armoury to replace Absolut, having lost the right to sell this Swedish vodka (in the United States in particular) in 1994.

Nevertheless, certain aspects are unchanged, and the idea of vodka as a comforter, a refuge from the inevitable horrors of real life, remains

Opposite
The new image of Russian vodka, neither Tsarist nor Communist.

Call me what you like, only give me some vodka.

— OLD RUSSIAN SAYING

dominant. In the middle of 1996 Alexander Ilyin, the last editor of *Pravda*, was accused by the paper's Greek owners of drinking too much. "When you work for a newspaper that has been falling apart for years," he said, "and your salary is just enough for a bottle of vodka, what else are you going to do?"

POLAND

Just as the Russians stake their claim, every Pole will tell you that vodka originated in Poland. The tradition of producing strong alcohol dates from the 8th century, when it was discovered that wine left to freeze during the winter resulted in a residue of stronger alcohol (water having a lower freezing point than alcohol). These early "distillers" were mainly pagan leaders, and the alcohol they produced was laced with herbs and applied to the body (rather than consumed) because of its medicinal benefits.

This vodka prototype was more widely produced by the 11th century, with nobles and monks having replaced pagans (Poland converted to Christianity in 966). While still perceived as medicinal, it was also being drunk.

The knowledge of distilling spirit from wine spread across Europe from France, reaching Poland between the 12th and 14th centuries. This new technology resulted in a drink termed *gorzalka*, an amalgamation of *gorzale wino,* meaning burnt or scorched wine. There was plenty of Polish wine ready to be scorched, with vineyards cultivated in the south, particularly around Zielona Gora and Cracow, as well as wine imported from Italy and Hungary. *Gorzalka*'s initial popularity also stemmed from its "medicinal" benefits, and it wasn't until the

Opposite

Not exactly what you'd call good mixers – a Russian aristocrat (left) and a Polish nobleman in 16th–century dress, from a 19th century German book of costume.

early 15th century that it became more firmly established as a social drink.

While it is impossible to specify an exact date when vodka first began to be produced (historical sources contradict each other), the earliest written reference dates from 1405, and Polish historians say this is the earliest such reference in Eastern Europe. Consequently, it is

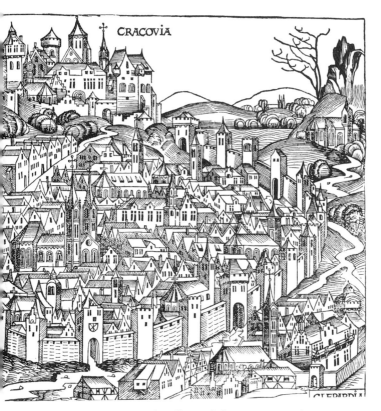

CRACOVIA

CLEPARDIA

claimed that the word vodka, and the concept, reached Russia from Poland – via Lithuania, Belarus and the Ukraine. The literal translation of vodka is little water, being the diminutive of *woda* meaning water (in Polish the "w" is pronounced as a "v"). This type of suffix was also used to indicate an improved version of the original. However, *vodka* was originally a

Above
Medieval Cracow, the traditional home of Poland's finest vodkas.

51

generic term that also encompassed various vodka-based remedies, fragrances, cleansers and even cosmetic preparations, while *gorzalka* was generally used to refer to the social drink. In his 1534 treatise *Herbal*, Polish herbalist Stefan Falimirz listed 72 herb vodkas which could be used to treat "different indispositions" and wrote that "vodka is used for washing the chin after shaving". He also described the distillation process and how the distillate was mixed with herbs and other flavourings.

Keep on drinking, for what does old age hold for you except a bag and a walking stick.

— **OLD POLISH SAYING**

By the early 15th century, and possibly earlier, grain was being used as a raw material for distillation. Cereals, particularly buckwheat and ale, were always a staple in the Slav diet, which made grain a logical alternative to distilling wine. Various grains were used for distillation, including wheat, buckwheat and oats, though rye was the most usual. Initially this vodka was single-distilled to a strength of around 15 per cent abv, and generally drunk diluted with water, following the tradition of diluting wine.

By the first half of the 16th century vodka was all set to begin its phenomenal rise as a social drink after King Jan Olbracht passed a statute in 1546, allowing all Poles to produce and sell alcohol. The response was immediate. By 1550 a significant amount of vodka was being distilled in Cracow (the Polish capital until 1596), as well as in Gdansk and Poznan, both important trading centres. Fulvius Ruggieri, an Italian who toured Poland in 1568, wrote to a friend in Rome giving precise details of the Polish distillation process. But the free-for-all only lasted until 1572, when the King reassessed the situation. The resulting new policy was that the gentry gained exclusive rights to distil and sell alcohol, a privilege for which they were of course taxed. Nevertheless, it was a golden opportunity, and by 1580 there were 49 "distilling pots" recorded in Poznan alone, while distilleries soon became a standard feature of country estates and monasteries.

"Breweries and distilleries have been built everywhere, and swallowed not only grain but also entire villages," commented the Reverend Hieronim Prowodowski in 1595. Nevertheless, even at this stage vodka was still being used by some for medicinal purposes. Indeed, a treatise entitled *Vodka or Gorzalka,* published in 1614 by the scientist Jurek Potanski, stated in its introduction that:

> *Though you've had vodka in Poland for so*
> *   long*
> *Its virtues, still, are fairly unknown*
> *So read this book all ye vodka-men*
> *To see how your health vodka can maintain.*

As the vodka trade became a major source of revenue for the gentry and the Crown, growing

Above
Beautiful antique bottles which were used for some of the spirits distilled at Lancut.

sales also offered further potential for taxation. This resulted in a special *czopowe* (tap tax) in the 17th century, which meant 10 per cent on the production and sale of vodka.

However, production techniques were still crude, as a method of refining vodka and removing all of the impurities remained elusive. Whatever distillers could not remove they tried to conceal, by adding aromatic oils and spices (Poland had long been on the trade route from Asia to Western Europe and Scandinavia), with honey also used as a sweetener. These practical measures helped to develop Poland's vast range of flavoured vodkas, the most eccentric specimen being *zmijowka*, prepared by marinading an adder in vodka for several weeks.

The most expensive vodka, and a status symbol amongst the gentry was Gdansk vodka, dating from the 16th century (and still produced in Poland as Goldwasser, meaning Gold Water). An extravagant recipe used anise-flavoured vodka as a basis for infusing ingredients such as pepper, gypsy rose, valerian root, sandalwood and rosewood. After a second distillation gold leaf was added, which was thought to have medicinal properties. "Silver Water" was also produced, presumably one rung below the Gold version in terms of prestige.

When the bosses start drinking the distillery runs dry.
— **OLD POLISH SAYING**

Gdansk was an immensely wealthy city, having been granted exclusive rights to Poland's maritime trade in the 15th century. From 1620 vodka licences were sold in Gdansk (which did not limit unofficial production), and Polish vodka was first exported from Gdansk in the 17th century to other European countries such as Denmark and England.

The Polish-Lithuanian Commonwealth, inaugurated in 1569, also helped to bring Zubrowka (see page 129) to the fore. The Polish royal circle's visits to Lithuania, via the Bialowieza Forest, entailed visiting the region's manor houses, where Zubrowka was offered as a local speciality. It charmed the royal palates, supplies were taken back to the capital, Cracow, and Zubrowka was soon established as a national favourite.

There was no such royal endorsement for Tatra vodka, although it was the Polish Highlander's equivalent of Zubrowka, using wild herbs collected in southern Poland's Tatra mountains. Developed during the 16th century, its principal ingredient was angelica, a herb said to relieve digestive, nervous, respiratory and circulation problems.

Krupnik (honey flavoured vodka) continued Poland's ancient mead tradition, by rerouting honey into vodka, to which cinnamon, cloves and ginger were also added. Just like mead, *krupnik* was frequently served hot, making it a popular winter drink with the gentry. A typical way to serve *krupnik* was from a punch bowl, in which it was briefly ignited to help fuse the flavours, while blowing out the flames was a popular party game. *Krupnik's* popularity reached a peak during the party season of Carnival, supposedly the last chance to have fun between Twelfth Night and the beginning of Lent on Ash Wednesday. Meanwhile, the popularity of *krupnik* was boosted still further by the legend of Prince Gedymin, who ruled 14th-century Lithuania. He attributed his recovery from a long illness to a prescription consisting entirely of *krupnik*.

Poland's tradition of aged vodka (which continues with the Starka brand) owes a debt to the popularity of *wegrzyn*, a dry white Tokay wine, which had been popular since Queen Jadwiga of Hungary came to the Polish throne in 1384. A traditional way for the gentry to celebrate the birth of a daughter was to fill empty Hungarian wine casks (made of oak) with rye vodka, which was laid down until the daughter's wedding day. That allowed plenty of time for the vodka to mature into a mellow, fragrant spirit. As an important family event, country weddings traditionally lasted three days, though no one was present for the entire duration; guests would celebrate, leave, return, leave and so on.

There aren't any ugly women, only too little vodka.
— **OLD POLISH SAYING**

Needless to say, vodka played a big part in Polish hospitality, and eating, drinking and dancing were usually taken to the limit, with every meal viewed as a social opportunity. In a country where the most revered characteristics, particularly among the gentry, were romanticism (with a great sense of honour and patriotism), together with a certain bravado, and of course extravagant hospitality, nothing less would do. This *modus vivendi* was continually being reinforced within the national consciousness – Poland was invaded so frequently that the threat of being dispossesed of property, if not slain, by the latest enemy was ever-present.

By the 17th century vodka was firmly established as the national drink, and consumed with gusto by each social class. The Frisian writer Verdun noted in 1672 that "even the greatest aristocrats enjoy vodka and take it with them wherever they travel". However, there wasn't always equality between the social classes when it came to quality, and the raw materials from which the vodka was distilled. Verdun adds that "The finest vodka is made from rye, and the worst is made from nettles."

Poland's finest vodka was established throughout Europe in the 17th century, when Polish distilling equipment was even exported to Russia. The first written Polish reference to vodka purely as a social drink dates from 1600. And it was in the 17th century that the word vodka became the standard reference used by everyone (replacing *gorzalka*).

Opposite
The palace of Jan III Sobieski at Wilanow, where Poland's first potatoes were grown.

The Polish vodka industry boomed after further technical advances in the 18th century, among them triple-distillation. This made for greater quality and strength, with vodka produced at around 70 per cent abv, and then diluted with water. Filtration improved as charcoal took over from earlier methods, and variety increased with more than 100 flavoured styles being produced.

The use of potatoes as a raw material was another 18th-century innovation. Potatoes arrived in Poland after King Jan III Sobieski returned from the Battle of Vienna in 1683, where the Polish army defeated the Turks. After

the battle the King saw potatoes for the first time at the Austrian emperor's palace, and was presented with some prize specimens. These were planted at Wilanow, Jan Sobieski's baroque summer residence on the edge of Warsaw (now a museum).

Potatoes were initially a novelty for the aristocracy, rather than a daily staple, and did not become widespread until Stanislaus Augustus Poniatowski came to the throne in 1764. Since he was also Elector of Saxony, Poniatowski invited Germans to settle on a

number of royal estates, and they began the more widespread cultivation of potatoes, by introducing them to Polish peasants. While potato vodka remains a speciality (using high-starch varieties cultivated in specific "micro-climates" along the Vistula river and Baltic coast), rye has remained the chief source of Polish vodka.

By the second half of the 18th century Polish vodka had established pre-eminence across Europe and Russia, with many new distilleries being founded. In Lvov (now part of the Ukraine) the JA Baczewski distillery was established in 1782 as one of Europe's largest operations, producing 123 styles of vodka, together with liqueurs, rum and arracks, which were exported to 20 overseas markets (the Polmos distillery at Starogard continues to distill JA Baczewski vodka).

In 1784, Lancut, Poland's oldest working distillery, was founded in the south-east of the country. It was established by Princess Lubomirska, principally to cater to her extravagant, bohemian lifestyle. The Lancut estate was originally acquired by the Lubomirski family at the end of the 17th century, complete with a baroque castle including stone ramparts and solid earthwork fortifications (useful features that resisted Swedish and Turkish sieges). Building the distillery was part of a general overhaul of the estate, with Princess Lubomirska reworking the

Opposite
The palatial Lancut, Poland's oldest working distillery, was built to satisfy the extravagant tastes of Princess Lubomirska

castle in a distinguished neoclassical style, while
also adding romantic pavilions and an
orangerie. (The castle is now a museum.
Another museum, housed in a classical 1830
manor house, traces the development of vodka
production at Lancut, as well as the history of
distillation in Poland.)

In 1830 Lancut passed into the Potocki
family, relatives of Princess Lubomirska, who
expanded the distillery and introduced many
specialist vodkas. The range also included
kosher vodka (reflecting Poland's large Jewish
community), which helped to establish even
higher standards throughout the industry.

At the beginning of the 19th century a
distillery built in Warsaw by Leon
Nowachowicz achieved a dominant position in
the vodka market. Then in 1846 a trader from
Gdansk, Aleksander Wilkenhausen, set up a
distillery in Starogard, where
Poland's first rectification plant
was established in 1871. Other
very successful enterprises were
Hartwig-Kantorowicz in Poznan,
while Warsaw saw J Fuch's distillery established
in 1856, followed by M Patsche in 1873, and
the Warsaw Rectification Co in 1889.

Vodka in excess, brain in recess.

— **OLD POLISH** SAYING

Gniezno (briefly capital of Poland in the 11th
century) was home to the Kasprowicz Distillery,
which was producing 88 vodkas and liqueurs by
the end of the 19th century. One of its most
popular styles was Gnesnania Boonekamp (still

produced in Poland), a digestif vodka using 23 herbs and spices.

A number of distilleries which now operate under the state-run Polmos banner, were also established in the 19th century. These include Bielsko-Biala in 1827, Zielona Gora in 1860, and Siedlce in 1896.

Opposite
The old distillery in the Polish town of Bielsko-Biala.

To maintain exemplary standards, a state monopoly overseeing all vodka production was established after World War I (when Poland regained independence having been partitioned by Prussia, Austro-Hungary and Russia in 1772). The state acquired the Warsaw Rectification Co, apart from which 17 privately owned distilleries operated in Poland. These were only licensed to produce flavoured vodka, while the monopoly

You can't sort anything out without vodka.
— **OLD POLISH SAYING**

retained exclusive rights to distil clear vodka and rectified spirit. This system operated until the outbreak of World War II, and the monopoly organization was re-established in Warsaw in 1945. In 1973 the monopoly was restructured when vodka production came under the government's newly formed Polmos organization.

Vodka's status as the national drink grew during the post-war era, partly because in terms of relative alcoholic strength, it was less expensive than wine and beer.

During the 1980s shortages of many foodstuffs and consumer goods were a part of daily life in Poland. Between 1981 and 1982 vodka too was rationed and only available using coupons. Ironically, even people who didn't drink vodka took up their allowance, as vodka could then be bartered for other foodstuffs and goods. The monthly vodka allowance was half a litre, though in "extraordinary" cases, such as weddings and baptisms, it was possible to be considered for an additional amount, on production of the necessary documentation. At this time vodka (as well as various foodstuffs

Above
Wooden casks for blending flavoured vodkas at the Zielona Gora distillery.

and consumer goods) was readily available in Pewex and Baltona, state-run shops that only accepted hard currency. But these shops were prohibitively expensive, and the majority of Poles had no hard currency. Needless to say, home distilling flourished, and by all estimates the level of vodka consumption did not actually decrease. A great boon in this respect was a certain Junior Chemistry Set, which suddenly became a best-seller, though not among children. Fortunately there were no shortages in this line.

In July 1991, following the democratic elections in 1989, Poland's Polmos distilleries became independent entities, though still ultimately government-owned. Privatizing the distilleries has been under consideration, but

their revenue is so valuable that if it goes ahead the government is expected to retain a 51 per cent interest in each distillery (with shares offered to employees). Rights to the classic vodka brands like Wyborowa and Zubrowka are divided between Agros and Polmos. Agros is the former state import/export monopoly, privatized in 1993, which originally registered the trademarks for export. Polmos, which now comprises 25 autonomous distilleries, holds the domestic market rights.

Each Polmos distillery currently holds a "no fee" licence to produce the classic vodka brands (individual distilleries are now named on the bottle label). Distilleries are also allowed to produce, export and own outright any new brands they develop. These new brands are

Above
Vats for rectified spirit at the Zielona Gora distillery.

Above
The distinctive retro-chic label of Poland's best-known brand.

generally more profitable, as the distilleries determine their own price-positioning, subject to approval by the Ministry of Finance, whereas classic brands have a fixed price. Meanwhile, 86 per cent of the retail price of a bottle of vodka is accounted for by various taxes. Not surprisingly, there has been a surge of NPD (New Product Development) resulting in an estimated total of a thousand Polish vodka brands currently on the market.

The development of the new brands, however, is a tremendous challenge because advertising is forbidden, and distribution is by wholesalers who operate on a regional basis. Actually getting a brand on to a retail shelf when there is so much competition means following up on endless numbers of small-scale and corner shop retailers, as large national retail/supermarket chains are not yet established. Needless to say, the number of brands on the market is expected to diminish.

Although the market is dominated by standard vodka, there is also a growing super-premium sector, with brands such as Krolewska launched by Zielona Gora, Chopin vodka from the Siedlce distillery, and Belweder (named after

Above and Left
A range of new vodkas produced in Poland, one of which features Frederic Chopin (left).

the palace in Warsaw) produced by Zyrardow. Packaging is far more design-conscious, a popular choice being a frosted glass bottle featuring a clear window in place of a label, through which a design such as Chopin's portrait can be seen, etched on the opposite side of the bottle.

Distilleries are also diversifying beyond vodka, with Zielona Gora and Poznan for instance, bottling bulk imported French brandy under their own brand names, while Cracow, Bielsko-Biala and Zielona Gora are extending their portfolios by producing other spirits such as gin. Agros is also active on the market, having launched wines, brandy and Scotch whisky brands through its subsidiary Torwin.

Polmos distilleries are also allowed to form partnerships with overseas companies, subject to government approval, though no actual equity can be sold. Lanique is the brand name of a partnership between Lancut distillery and a British company, Euro Class. The range includes Rose Petal vodka (flavoured with attar of roses, it was very popular earlier this century), and fruit vodkas like plum, orange, lemon and cherry. Similarly, Jozefow distillery has an agreement with IDV (International Distillers & Vintners, the drinks division of

Grand Metropolitan), which resulted from the ban on imported vodka imposed by the Polish government between 1989 and July 1995. This ban was intended to protect domestic vodka from an expected onslaught by imported vodka brands. Consequently, Smirnoff Red has been distilled at Jozefow since the spring of 1994 for the Polish market. This was in a sense a homecoming. When Pierre Smirnoff fled the Russian revolution in 1917, he initially established a distillery in Lvov (then part of Poland, now part of the Ukraine), before moving to Paris in 1922. In addition to Polmos distilleries, several private enterprises have been licensed since 1989, though their production levels are a fraction of Polmos'.

Above
Old price lists from the museum at Lancut.

Opposite
The patriarchal face of Pierre Smirnoff, who fled the Russian Revolution for Poland.

Opposite
*One of the kosher
vodkas produced by
Poland's Polmos
distilleries.*

Overall, Polish vodka production totals an estimated 50 million cases annually, of which around 80 per cent are clear styles. In terms of volume, the leading Polmos distilleries include Poznan, Zielona Gora, Starogard Gdansk, Cracow and Wroclaw. Consumer perception is such that Zielona Gora and Poznan (Poland's

Vodka in the morning flows like cream.
— **OLD POLISH SAYING**

largest producer of rectified spirit) are thought to produce the best-quality vodka. This is partly because both distilleries supplied export markets during the Communist era, when any product destined for export was assumed to be of superior quality.

The domestic vodka market accounts for 35-40 million cases annually, with vodka taking an estimated 80 per cent of total alcohol sales in Poland. While the government is continually campaigning for moderate drinking, Poland still has one of the world's highest rates of consumption, at eight litres of pure alcohol per person per annum.

KOSHER VODKA

The vogue for kosher vodka in Poland emerged at the end of the 1980s, after Zygmunt Nissenbaum (a survivor of the Warsaw Ghetto, and founder of the Nissenbaum Foundation)

initiated the first post-war production of kosher vodka through a joint-venture agreement with Polmos. Starting in 1987, the agreement was due to run for 30 years, but just two years later the democratic elections were held, bringing about the possibility of private production. Consequently, the Nissenbaum

Foundation has developed its wholly-owned Nisskosher range of kosher vodka.

Production began in 1992, after researching traditional Jewish recipes and gaining the approval of organizations such as the Union of Orthodox Jewish Congregations of America. A range of six varieties of clear vodka spans potato and grain styles, with a herbal vodka called Dziegielowka, all distilled at the Nissenbaum's own distillery in Bielsko-Biala. Profits derived from Nisskosher vodka go towards the restoration of Jewish cemeteries and cultural monuments in Poland.

The Nissenbaum Foundation is unique in Poland in that it produces only kosher vodka at its distillery, as opposed to various Polmos distilleries, including Zielona Gora and Bielsko-Biala, which produce certified kosher vodka as part of their overall repertoire.

While many distillers would claim that all vodka is pure, it was a sense of enhanced purity

The best things in Poland are vodka from Gdansk, gingerbread from Torun, a maiden from Cracow and shoes from Warsaw.
— **OLD POLISH SAYING**

associated with the word "kosher" (as well as the innovation itself) that helped to propel kosher vodka as a consumer phenomenon in Poland.

The stringent regulations applied to the production of kosher vodka mean higher

Left
A rabbi giving his blessing to a bottle of koszerna ("kosher") vodka.

production costs. Contracts granting kosher certificates are awarded on an annual basis, with rabbis checking that all rules are observed. Any machinery involved may only be used to produce kosher vodka in an uninterrupted process from the still to the bottle. Water must come from a source where the land is uninhabited and not used for agricultural purposes. Bottles must be brand new each time and arrive wrapped in foil, the entire process being mechanized to prevent bottles being touched by human hands.

SWEDEN

Over the past four centuries the third Great Power in Northern Europe, along with Russia and Poland, was Sweden which intermittently ruled many of its neighbours. Indeed Norway did not gain its independence until 1905. Not unexpectedly, Sweden too developed a vodka-culture of its own, albeit one severely limited since the mid-19th century by a significant element of state control, the result of the country's strong temperance movement.

By the 14th century what was called *brannwein* had reached Scandinavia, as we know from the discovery in Denmark of a still dating from that era. A contemporary seer known as Holy Birgitta even described how to distil spirits in the course of her revelations, a further indication of the way that in Sweden, as elsewhere in Europe, monasteries were the major distillers.

As in the other regions of Northern and Eastern Europe, *brannwein* was originally thought of as a medicine. According to a 15th-century Swedish document, it could cure more than 40 ailments, including headache, head lice, kidney stones and toothache, as well as being "good for women who are infertile".

By the late 16th century, however, it was being sold at a high price as a luxury beverage. When water-cooled stills came into use the

Opposite
A winter sunset over frozen Stockholm. The perfect time to retire indoors for a warming vodka and smorgasbord.

Opposite
The Swedish state liquor monopoly has come a long way – from puritanical rationing to free-flowing international iconic status. The label opposite was designed by Andy Warhol.

price gradually fell, so that by the middle of the 17th century *brannwein* had become very much a people's drink – and a highly important source of revenue for the Swedish crown. But already Sweden's own form of puritanism, which was to come into full flower in the 19th century, was being felt. In 1683 the governor of northern Sweden reported that: "Both soldiers and farmers are drawn to drinking *brannvin* and in this way consume their health and welfare and neglect both culture and service." And in the mid-18th century the famous botanist, Carl von Linnaeus, warned that "*Brannvin* has the same effect that a whip does on a mare. It causes an immediate charge but does not boost the horse's strength."

As a result of this pressure the state tried intermittently to ban or control the production and sale of *brannvin*, but the need for revenue proved more important than considerations of health or morality. By 1756, indeed, it was estimated that there were 180,000 stills in Sweden, one for every 10 inhabitants. Culturally it was so important that there were special names for the nip drinkers took before hunting, fishing, walking or even before going to bed (this was called a *nattsup*, echoing the English nightcap).

Production gradually evolved, potatoes were introduced as a raw material and technical improvements were made. These included Coffey's continuous still as well as refinements

Opposite
With Glasnost,
Absolut's advertising
team rediscovered
Russia.

such as pre-heaters and condensers, and the "Pictorius' Dephlegmator". This useful device condensed much of the steam and increased the strength of the alcohol-laden vapour to 80 per cent. As a result of these changes and stills becoming more efficient, the number of stills fell from 173,000 in 1829 to a mere 33,000 in 1853.

In the late 19th century the Swedes had developed the idea of drinking ice-cold vodka with food. Restaurants presented customers with a 'canteen', a special holder with up to six taps. These canteens offered several different iced vodkas including specially purified spirit and others blended with orange and caraway seeds, to be drunk with *smorgasbord*, the Swedish equivalent of *zakuski* (see page 163). But abstentionists objected to paying the same price for their food as drinkers. So a charge was instituted for every shot. Sadly, it proved impossible to rely on drinkers' honesty and as a result, the canteen – affectionately known as Fritz – disappeared into alcoholic history.

Unfortunately for the Swedes, the forces of temperence became stronger after the birth of the Swedish Temperance Society in 1837 – not surprisingly, given the degree of drunkeness associated with life in the country. By 1860 home distillation had been forbidden and the number of distilleries dropped to 564 (but production actually increased from 24 million litres in 1860 to 43 million litres 10 years later as these were commercial distilleries).

The temperance grip tightened after World War I, with the emergence of Vin & Spirit, a state monopoly covering the production and sale of alcoholic beverages. These were subject to huge excise taxes and sold under extremely restrictive conditions – for nearly half a century drinkers had to present a ration book to obtain liquor. All these restrictions, similar to those operating in Norway and Finland, were founded on the belief that the Swedes could not be trusted with strong drink, and would automatically get drunk rather than enjoy liquor in a civilized way. With Sweden's entry into the European Union in 1995 the constraints were relaxed.

Meanwhile, however, the company Vin & Spirit resurrected an old brand, repackaged and reformulated it under the name of Absolut, (see page 88) and found itself with a major international success on its hands.

FINLAND, BALTIC STATES & UKRAINE

At some time or another over the past 500 years one or other of the Swedish, Polish and Russian empires has dominated all the other now-independent countries in the region – Finland, Norway, Estonia, Latvia and Lithuania, while Ukraine and Belarus were for so long part of Russia or the Soviet Union that they had very little opportunity to develop their own styles of vodka, their own vodka-culture.

Nevertheless some distinctive elements did exist and are slowly re-emerging following the break-up of the Soviet Union. The Ukrainians, for instance, had their own word for vodka: *gorilka*, meaning flaming, derived from the word *goriti* (to flame up). Ukrainian vodka was famous as early as the mid-17th century even in Moscow. There it was known as Cherkasskoe vino, named after Cherkassy, close to Chigirin, then capital of the Ukraine. It was made from wheat, and the Russians alleged that the vodka, brought to Moscow by local Cossacks, who did not know how to purify the spirit, was of such poor quality that it was sold only in low-grade

The first glass is usually drunk to everybody's health. The second for pleasure, the third for insolence, the last for madness.

— **OLD LATVIAN SAYING**

taverns. Unlike the Muscovites, they did not have birch forests from which to make the charcoal that was so essential in purifying Russian vodka.

But the tradition remains and an excellent Ukrainian brand called Gorilka is still being made under the supervision of experts from Moscow. Unfortunately it is possible that any declaration of alcoholic independence would mean the lowering of the brand's quality. The same does not appear to be true of the vodkas re-emerging from Estonia and Latvia since their declarations of independence in 1991.

More typical is the story of vodka in Latvia. In 1900 the Latvians organized a state distillery which started producing 600,000 buckets of vodka a year, most of it from potatoes. The distillery was nationalized following the Russian invasion in 1940 and extended to produce other spirits, including the famous Black Balsam. Since Latvia regained its independence the company has been partially privatized, athough the state still retains 60 per cent of the shares. It now produces six vodkas, Kristaldzidrais, Rigas Orginalais, Favorits, Zelta, Rigalya and Monopols. All are sold at 40 per cent and produced from two types of rectified spirit based on local grain. The company claims that the last two are the equivalent quality of Absolut and Smirnoff.

Finland, which gained its independence from Russia in 1919, resembles Sweden in showing

Above
Finlandia vodka at the bottling stage. The distinctive "iced" bottle is an important element of the brand image.

how political independence and a tradition of distillation involving pure native water, can be transmuted into international commercial success. In the past even the super-nationalistic Pokhlebkin was forced to acknowledge the quality of Finnish vodka: "Even the exquisite Finnish vodka Finlandia, which uses rye grain and rye malt exclusively, has a taste which is distinctly different from Russian vodka... Finlandia is extremely natural, and there is no doubt about the use of rye in its preparation, since the Finnish makers are utterly scrupulous." However, he went on, "Finlandia still cannot stand comparison with Moscow vodka. This is because Finnish vodka uses Vasa

84

rye, the grains of which are heavier and cleaner than those of Russian rye, and which do not possess the characteristic rye taste of the Russian cereal."

Finlandia, Absolut's principal rival as an internationally marketed "Scandinavian" vodka, is the heir to a long tradition. Some 400 years ago Finnish mercenaries returning from fighting in Southern Europe brought home with them the know-how to produce vodka. By the end of the 17th century vodka, usually distilled in home stills, had almost entirely replaced beer as the national drink. But the origins of the modern Finnish vodka industry can be traced back to the decision made in the 1880s to set up a new factory to produce yeast at Rajamaki Manor, some 30 miles from Helsinki, a spot notable for the purity of the local water.

Rajamaki soon became the country's biggest distillery, but suffered from Finland's period of prohibition between the wars. It was revived to produce alcohol for "Molotov cocktails" – primitive anti-tank devices consisting of bottles filled with inflammable alcohol which proved surprisingly successful when the Soviets invaded Finland in late 1939. Since the war the distillery has been repeatedly modernized and enlarged, and is now the source of Finlandia, a story told on page 137.

If they raise the price of vodka to the price of a suit, which would you buy, vodka or a suit?
Vodka, naturally. Why would I need such an expensive suit?
— **OLD LATVIAN SAYING**

THE DIASPORA

The Russian Revolution led to the dispersal of the Russian merchant classes, including those who had run the country's major vodka distilleries, and this proved to be the origin of what might be called the "vodkas of the diaspora". The most obvious case is Smirnoff, its story recounted on page 91, but in recent years another brand, Gorbatschow (see page 139), has begun to spread from Germany, where the family took refuge after 1917. The success of Smirnoff – for some years the world's largest-selling spirit until it was overtaken by Bacardi, another drink made by refugees from a Communist revolution – has naturally bred hordes of imitators. These come from dozens of countries, from Italy to Cyprus, largely to supply cheap neutral spirit to be sold as the base of mixers for the tourists from Northern European countries.

The resulting brands can be divided into two main categories (although none of them is worth much attention in terms of inherent qualities). There are those with traditional Russian names, like Tolstoy and Alexander Nevski, designed to lure the uninitiated into believing that they are drinking the "real stuff". The other group of equally unremarkable spirits is made by firms like Gordon's and Tanqueray as what is known as a "line extension of a

Left

This brand was introduced to Germany by refugees from the Russian Revolution who originally distilled in St Petersburg.

famous brand name". They are merely cashing in, sometimes quite successfully, on the fame of their other spirits. To the true vodka connoisseur these are merely irritants, for by swamping the market they conceal the qualities provided by real vodkas.

There is, however, one other tiny category, the "tongue-in-cheek" brands, which deserve at least a short mention. The first, made by a small British brewer, Greenall's, was Vladivar, "the vodka from Varrington" – Warrington being the small town in Lancashire where it was distilled. To the infinite disgust of the Russians, their advertisements featured such phenomena as parades on Red Square. The brand was immensely successful and sold to a bigger firm. But now Greenall's have come up with the most tastelessly named Black Death, which we simply do not have the heart to condemn. And it doesn't taste bad either.

Opposite
The home of
Absolut vodka in
the small Swedish
town of Ahus.

ABSOLUT

The story of Absolut is uniquely ironic: invented in the late 1800s, it was resurrected a century later by an organization whose principal purpose was to ensure that the Swedes did not drink too much, and within just a few years it had become one of the world's greatest marketing successes. Absolut was dreamed up by one Lars Olsson Smith, Sweden's so-called liquor king who made and lost a number of fortunes fighting the official retail drinks

monopolies in the latter half of the 19th century. In 1879 he introduced an "absolutely pure" vodka relying on the rectifications made possible by continuous distilling equipment.

Lars Olsson Smith died penniless in 1913, and for 65 years Absolut remained dormant, owned by Vin & Spirit, the Swedish state liquor monopoly. When the time came to celebrate the brand's centenary, the management had the brilliant idea of exploiting Sweden's reputation for cleanliness,

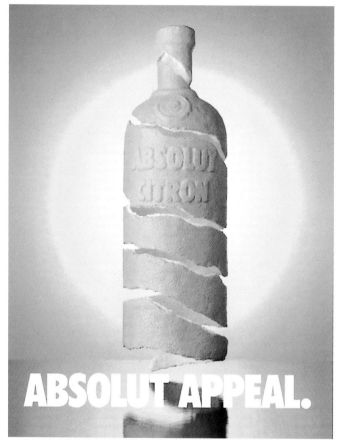

health and purity: they modelled the brand new Absolut bottle on an old medicine bottle, using a special translucent glass and a label which was not stuck on to the glass but actually engraved in it. Thanks to the inspired efforts of salesman

Michel Roux (of Carillon Importers, a subsidiary of International Distillers & Vintners), and some exceptionally elegant and witty advertising, associating the brand with every fashionable icon of the period, most obviously Andy Warhol, the brand became a totem of the 1980s in the United States.

By 1985 it was the country's biggest-selling imported vodka and since then has spread further: by 1995 millions of cases were being sold in 85 countries. It has since been reinforced by three other vodka products, Absolut Kurant, Absolut Citron and Absolut Peppar.

Absolut is made from grain in a single distillery in the small southern Swedish town of Ahus. It is rectified in four separate columns, three removing impurities, the fourth concentrating the spirit. A very little lower-strength spirit is added to provide the right degree of character.

SMIRNOFF

Smirnoff is the best-selling vodka in the world, and the clever way in which it was promoted in the two decades after the war, above all in the United States, transformed vodka from a relative curiosity into an internationally accepted spirit, suitable for mixing with a wide variety of soft drinks and other liquids, such as canned and packaged and fresh tomato juice, and bouillon.

Opposite
A pun which emphasises the ap'peel' of Absolut's lemon-flavoured vodka.

The Smirnov (as it was originally spelt) family had established itself in Moscow in the early 19th century. In the years after 1862, when all previous monopoly rights to the distillation of vodka were removed at the same time as the abolition of serfdom, the genius of the family, Piotr Arsenyevitch, built the firm up into the biggest in Russia – making his family one of the richest in the country. He bought out his cousins' stake in a rival family firm and by the time he died in 1898 Smirnov was established as supplier to the Tsar and was producing nearly

3,500,000 cases a year in the country's largest vodka distillery.

Nevertheless even before the 1917 revolution the family business was in decline. Ownership had passed to one of Piotr's daughters-in-law, Eugenia who went to live in Italy, eventually marrying an Italian. The 1917 revolution inevitably entailed the confiscation of the family business. One member of the family, Vladimir, was entrusted with the brand name, its production formula, and some of its cash, but failed to re-establish the brand despite heroic efforts. He first opened a distillery in Istanbul, then in Poland, before finally settling in France in 1928 where he set up a distillery, first near Paris, and then in Nice. While living in France he changed his own surname to Smirnoff and that of the company to Pierre Smirnoff in honour of his respected father, Piotr Arsenyevitch.

Rudolph Kunett, who under his former name of Kukhesh, had supplied the Smirnoff family with alcohol before 1917, bought the North American rights to Smirnoff while working for Helena Rubenstein. That was in late 1933, just before prohibition was repealed. He, too, failed and by the end of the decade had sold out to John Martin of the then-small liquor firm of Heublein.

In the years after the war Martin transformed the drink into the most fashionable of mixers. His first success was with the Moscow Mule.

Opposite above
The Smirnov Distillery at 2 Piatnitskaya Street in Moscow, the pride of the Smirnov Company, later turned into a garage at the time of the Russian Revolution.
Opposite below
The Smirnov stand at the 1896 Nizhny Novgorod Exhibition where Alexander III, on tasting Smirnov vodka, appointed them purveyors to the Imperial Court.

Opposite
The young Woody
Allen enjoying a
Moscow Mule with
copper-coated
blonde bombshell
Monique Van
Vooren.

This mixture of vodka and ginger beer was invented by accident to shift the otherwise unsaleable ginger beer brewed by Jack Morgan, owner of a Los Angeles bar called the Cock and Bull; it was sold in copper tankards which a local lady was equally unable to shift.

At first, it was sold on its lack of positive characteristics as "Smirnoff White Whisky. No taste. No Smell", but this essentially negative appeal was soon replaced by such slogans as "It leaves you breathless". The advertising has always been adventurous, pitched, successfully, at the young.

But Smirnoff still bases its appeal on purity. It is double-distilled in a process lasting 24 hours – the special, patented filtration process, involving charcoal made exclusively from hardwoods – and thus, by definition, resulting in a lack of positive characteristics.

In 1951 Heublein acquired the world rights to Smirnoff from Vladimir's widow, Tatiana, and the next year licensed the British rights to Gilbey's. In 1983 the group into which Gilbey's had been absorbed, International Distillers and Vintners, bought Heublein, and thus Smirnoff. This is now one of the biggest-selling distilled spirits in the world, with sales of 15 million cases in 1995. Over the years Smirnoff has expanded its range from the basic Red to the stronger Blue and now Black, distilled in Moscow in pot-stills, using the original recipe devised by Piotr Arsenyevitch.

NOTED STARS WOODY ALLEN AND MONIQUE VAN VOOREN ENJOY THEIR SMIRNOFF MULES TOGETHER

THIS IS THE DRINK THAT IS...THE SMIRNOFF MULE

Give a Mule party! You couldn't serve a smarter drink. For a cool, refreshing Mule made with Smirnoff and 7-Up' is a choice you can start with and stay with. Only crystal clear Smirnoff, filtered through 14,000 pounds of activated charcoal, blends so perfectly with 7-Up. So follow the rule when mixing the Mule. Make it with *Smirnoff!*

Smirnoff Mule Recipe:
Jigger of Smirnoff over ice.
Add juice of ¼ lime. Fill Mule
mug or glass with 7-Up to
taste. Delicious.

Set of 6 Mule mugs—$3.00
Send check or money order
payable to Smirnoff Mule,
Department J, P. O. Box 225,
Bklyn. N.Y 11202

Always ask for Smirnoff It leaves you breathless'
VODKA

CHAPTER TWO

BRAND DIRECTORY

THERE ARE LITERALLY THOUSANDS OF BRANDS OF VODKA ON THE MARKET, MADE IN DOZENS OF COUNTRIES THE WORLD OVER. IN THIS DIRECTORY, WE CONCENTRATE ON THE NAMES WHICH DESERVE THE ATTENTION OF TRUE VODKA-LOVERS.

Vodkas divide into two broad types: the mass of vodkas designed as a neutral alcoholic base for long drinks of every description; and those designed as a true drinking experience, with the same subtleties of aroma and flavour as other "serious" drinks. We have made a clear distinction between the two types by placing more emphasis on the "characterful" entries, providing a more detailed description of their qualities. Nevertheless, within the broadly "neutral" brands there are a few more interesting names – most obviously Smirnoff – which are based on the jealously guarded secret recipes taken into exile by Russian distillers after the Revolution. We hope to have included these worthwhile names, but make no apology if many other brands are not.

Opposite
The real thing – authentic Russian vodkas, such as these, are in increasing demand by connoisseurs.

RUSSIA

Cristall. Produced at Moscow's Cristall Distillery, considered the country's finest. Hint of grain, light and elegant but without much character and a tingling aftertaste.

Krepkaya. The name means strong. One of the finest of the stronger vodkas with distinctive personality, created especially for cocktails. Engaging, grainy spicy nose, reminiscent of spiced pears, with an attractive grainy flavour balancing the burn (which is less than expected from such a strong vodka). 56 per cent.

Kubanskaya. Stemming from the Russian Cossacks, who lived in the Kuban lowlands in the south of Russia. They made their own vodka with a delicate bouquet, produced according to an original recipe which includes a slightly bitter undertone.

Kremlyovskaya. Being the official drink at the Kremlin is quite a tag to have. It is distilled at a new distillery just outside Moscow, triple-distilled from grain spirit and filtered through charcoal. 37.5 per cent. Also Kremlyovskaya lemon, pepper, and blackcurrant flavoured line extensions. 37.5 per cent.

Left
*Limonnaya, with
the lemon providing
a classic addition to
the vodka.*

Limonnaya. Mild and smooth lemon vodka. Grain spirit flavoured with fresh lemon peel infusion with a little sugar added, slightly burning taste and fresh lemon fragrance.

Moskovskaya. A grain vodka. Named after the capital city, where it was first produced in the Grand Duchy of Moscow and exported to other Russian principalities. Also available is Moskovskaya Limon.

Opposite
Moskovskaya.
old-fashioned label,
old-fashioned vodka
- and none the
worse for that.

Moskovskaya Cristall. Produced at Russia's most renowned Cristall Distillery in Moscow. Light grainy flavour followed by a considerable burn, harshness and hint of bitterness.

Maccahapa Zarskaya Datscha. In 1896 Tsar Nicholas II built a vast wine cellar to provide for his summer residence in the village of Massandra, in Yalta, Crimea. In addition to wines produced on the estate, vodka is also distilled.

Okhotnichaya. Popular with hunters and outdoor types, it is produced from grain spirits flavoured with port and infusions of ginger, roots of tormentil and angelica, cloves, black and red pepper, juniper berry, coffee, seeds of star anise and orange and lemon peel. 45 per cent.

Pertsovka. Nut-brown, grain spirit taking its colour from infusions of red and black pepper pods and cubeb berries, has a long aftertaste. Peter the Great allegedly seasoned his vodka with pepper, now it is included. Burning, bitter taste and slightly spicy aroma. 35 per cent.

Pshenichnaya. A good quality vodka made from 100 per cent wheat. The name means "wheat". 40 per cent.

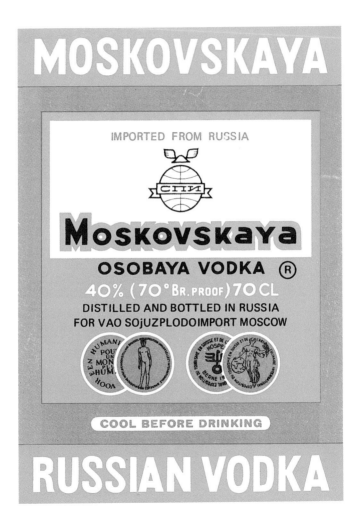

Above
Vodka from Siberia should benefit from the
region's icy-clean rivers and birch forests.

Above
Starka, a worthy example of a Russian oak-aged
vodka. This one is flavoured with leaves.

Opposite
This is a potato
spirit distilled
according to a
15th-century
recipe.

Russkaya. Filtered through birch-tree charcoal and quartz sand, a style first produced in the 15th century made from potatoes and flavoured with a small amount of cinnamon.

Sibirskaya. Originating from Siberia, distilled from winter wheat that survives the extreme Siberian frosts and repeatedly filtered through taiga birch tree charcoal. Slightly aniseed nose, repeated on the palate with aniseed/liquorice tones, smooth but a good bite too. 42 per cent.

Smirnoff Black. Embodies the traditional style of Imperial Russian vodka, dating back to the distillation methods of Ivan Smirnov in the 1800s, made from the highest quality neutral Russian grain spirit, distilled in a copper-pot-still to preserve the grain's natural flavours and mellow quality. Filtered through Siberian Silver Birch. Light, rye tone with nice creamy charcoal overtones, tangy and ends good and sharp, albeit with a slight burn.

Starka. The name means old vodka, grain spirit flavoured with an infusion of leaves from apple and pear trees grown in the Crimea, as well as brandy and port, with a barely perceptible touch of wine. 43 per cent.

Stolichnaya. *Stolitsa* means "capital city", distilled in Moscow, this is Russia's best-known export brand, and cited as a premier example of Russian vodka with a little sugar added. Good, oily nose with creamed corn carrying through on to the palate, good warmth without any rough edges. Also Stolichnaya Limon and Pepper (see Pertsovka).

Stolichnaya Cristall. The deluxe version produced at the Cristall distillery. Grainy nose, slightly metallic, oily flavour and a pronounced burn and acrid note in the aftertaste.

Stolbovaya. Grain vodka available as Original, Pepper and Anis.

Stolovaya. An ideal vodka to serve with food. 50 per cent.

Ultraa. Uses the pure and "oxygen-rich" waters of Lake Ladoga and Russian grain. It is presented in cobalt blue glass bottles and promoted as a reflection of the new Russia, without Tsarist or Stalinist imagery, although the recipe is based on one used for the Tsar's imperial palaces. 37.5 per cent.

Yubileynaya. Vodka flavoured with brandy, honey and other flavourings.

Opposite
Pepper is the classic Russian additive, helping the vodka meld with many traditional dishes.

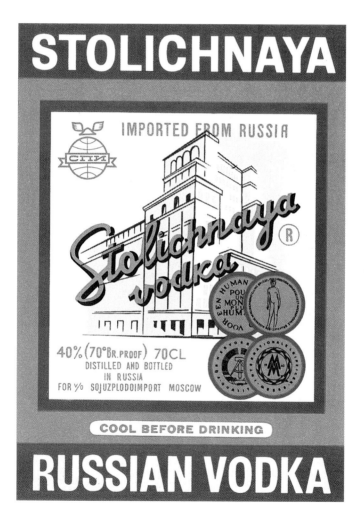

Zubrovka. A greenish-yellow vodka distilled from the infusion of "sweet grass" with a herbaceous, mild and slightly burning flavour, combining liquorice, toffee and cough medicine.

Opposite
Stolly: now being promoted by IDV as the authentic Russian vodka (which it is).

POLAND

JA Baczewski's Vodka Monopolowa.
Made under licence by Polmos Starogard-Gdansk to a Baczewski family recipe. Originally distilled in Lvov in 1782 (then part of Poland).

Baltic. Potato vodka, named after the Baltic coastline where high-starch potatoes are cultivated specifically for vodka. Special Baltic has the addition of rye spirit matured for a couple of years in oak casks.

Opposite
The Poles are making a considerable effort to persuade drinkers that potato vodkas can be exceptional.

Barowa. Grain spirit, produced by Polmos Poznan.

Belveder. Developed by Polmos Zyrardow, and named after an 18th-century neoclassical palace in Warsaw. Smooth, elegant and lightly creamy.

Black Currant (Wodka z Czarnej Porzeczki).
Semi-sweet, fruity vodka with a pronounced blackcurrant flavour. 30 per cent.

Bols. Produced and bottled under licence of Bols Royal Distilleries, Netherlands in Poland.

Chopin. Premium rye vodka named after Poland's composer, Frederic Chopin, launched by Polmos Siedlce in 1993. Full-bodied and extremely smooth.

Cytrynowka. Lemon peel and lemon tree leaves harvested at a special time provide this full-bodied vodka with a gentle lemon flavour.

Czardasz. Paprika-flavoured vodka. Smooth aroma and a gently piquant flavour.

Extra Zytnia. Rye vodka with a small addition of apple spirit and aromatic fruit ingredients. One of the most popular Polish rye vodkas this has a light, grainy nose, smooth subtle sweetness, though dry and exquisitely light on the palate, with overtones of its aromatic fruit ingredients, and retaining its rye taste. 40 per cent. Specjalna Zytnia is the deluxe version made from the best quality rectified rye spirit with a dry, subtle, rye flavour. 45 per cent

Right
A gentle,
lemon -flavoured
spirit.
Opposite
One of the best
Polish rye vodkas.

TRADE MARK

Polmos

GNESNANIA
BOONEKAMP

GNIEŻNIEŃSKA
GORZKA ŻOŁĄDKOWA

PREPARED FROM 23 KINDS OF HERBS AND SPICES
ACCORDING TO AN OLD RECIPE FROM GNIEZNO

40% alc./vol.   750 ml
PRODUCED AND BOTTLED IN POLAND BY POLMOS-POZNAN

Gnesnania Boonekamp. A "bitters" style vodka, flavoured with 23 herbs and spices extracted with diluted rectified spirit. Said to be an excellent digestif.

TRADE MARK

Polmos

The State Spirits Monopoly in Poland

JARZĘBIAK

Rowan Flavored Vodka

40% vol.   50 cl

PRODUCED AND BOTTLED IN POLAND

Opposite
This is a herbal
vodka generally
drunk as a digestif.
Left
A complicated recipe
based on the use of
rowan berries
produces this
brand of vodka.

Gold-Wasser. Based on twice rectified spirit with over a dozen herbs and spices and tiny flakes of real gold, made according to a 16th-century recipe from its hometown of Gdansk. A digestif style, with a rich, full-bodied palate with notes of liquorice, rhubarb, fruit compote, particularly cooked oranges.

Herszl. Grain vodka with a delicate aroma from fruit distillates. 39 per cent.

115

Jazz. Rye vodka produced by Polmos Starogard-Gdansk.

Jarzebiak. A blend of rectified spirit, infusion distillate and rowan spirit made from rowan berries picked after the first frost. Acrid berry taste mollified and refined by a small addition of sugar, well-seasoned wine, essence of figs, raisins and dried plums, matured in oak casks.

Jarzebiak na Winiaku. The deluxe version of the above with the addition of aged wine distillate. 43 per cent

Krakus. Twice-rectified rye spirit, using selected varieties of rye, and additionally refined for exceptional smoothness. Named after Cracow, the former capital of Poland.

Krolewska. Super-premium grain vodka launched by Polmos Zielona Gora. Delicate character made from the finest rectified spirit. Stained-glass window effect of the bottle utilizes coats of arms of some of the most distinguished Polish dynasties. Red capsule is 40 per cent, blue capsule is 42 per cent.

Opposite
One of the rare vodkas made to resemble traditional honey-based spirits.

Krupnik. Flavoured with spices and wild bees' honey gathered in the forests. Dating from the 16th century, this represents a continuation of Poland's ancient mead tradition. Outstanding bouquet of honey and spices. Can be served hot.

Polmos

Krupnik

Old Polish Honey Liqueur

*Prepared from bee honey and
various spices and aromatic
herbs according to Polish recipes many hundred years old*

40% vol.   70 cl

PRODUCE OF POLAND   ZIELONA GÓRA

Lanique. Brand name of a partnership between Polmos Lancut and a British company ECC Trading. The range includes Wyborowa, Cherry, Lemon, Plum (32 per cent), Orange and Rose Petal (flavoured with attar of roses, which used to be a very popular style at the beginning of the century).

LANIQUE

CYTRYNKA
LEMON VODKA

40%VOL   e 0.7L

MADE ONLY FROM NATURAL INGREDIENTS
PRODUCED AND BOTTLED IN LANCUT, POLAND

Polmos

POLISH
LUXURY
VODKA

LUKSUSOWA

100% NEUTRAL
SPIRITS

DISTILLED
FROM SELECT
POTATOES

0,75 l

40% obj.

PRODUCED
AND
BOTTLED
IN POLAND

ZIELONA GÓRA-POLAND

Luksusowa. The name means deluxe, and it is made from potato spirit. Exceptionally smooth, creamy, with a hint of sweetness. 45 per cent.

Mysliwska. Dry juniper vodka flavoured with rectified juniper distillate together with herbs and juniper berries gathered from selected species in Polish forests. Definite juniper taste, typically drunk by hunters. 45 per cent.

Opposite and left
Two vodkas from a range made by an Anglo-Polish venture.

Nisskosher. Brand of kosher vodkas produced by the Nissenbaum Family Foundation at a privately owned distillery in Bielsko-Biala. The range includes Dziegielowka (herbal vodka), Kosher (grain vodka), Purim (potato vodka with added fruit distillates), Szabasowka (potato vodka) and Trojka (potato vodka).

Pieprzowka. Based on twice-rectified spirit with a dry spicy flavour obtained from Turkish pepper, black pepper and other ingredients giving a prolonged aftertaste.

Polish Pure Spirit (Spirytus Rektyfikowany). Poland is one of Europe's major producers of rectified spirit, using grain and potatoes. Rectified spirit is the basic component of Polish vodka, and Polish Pure Spirit is intended for using with mixers. Completely neutral. 57, 79 and 96 per cent.

Opposite
Classic pepper
vodka.
Above
Hair-raisingly
strong pure spirit
which is useful for
very long drinks.

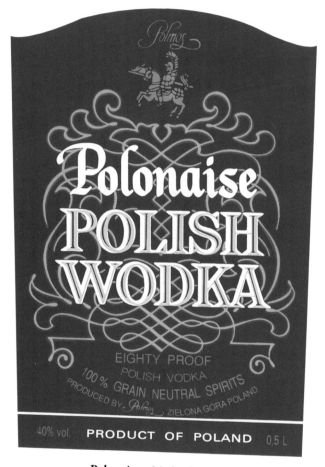

Polonaise. Made from rectified rye spirit, which comes through smoothly on the palate. White Label 40 per cent, Blue Label 50 per cent.

Polowa. Grain vodka which receives additional filtration through charcoal for a particularly delicate flavour. Produced by Polmos Poznan.

Premium. Being distilled four times gives this grain spirit vodka an exceptional smoothness. Produced by Polmos Poznan. Premium Lemon and Pepper are flavoured line extensions.

DISTILLED FROM GRAIN

PRODUCED AND BOTTLED IN POLAND

50% alc./vol. POLMOS POZNAŃ 0,75 dm³

Soplica. An ancient Polish vodka, named after an old family of country squires in Lithuania, as described in the epic poem "Pan Tadeusz" by the Romantic Polish poet Adam Mickiewicz. Dry vodka with a delicate taste made from doubly rectified spirit with a small addition of old wine distillate, well-seasoned apple spirit made from aromatic winter apples and fruit infusions. Matured in oak casks for several years to provide an exceptionally smooth apple-wine flavour.

Spodka. Produced from potato spirit by Polmos Starogard-Gdansk distillery. Creamy, smooth, rounded, and a nice degree of heat without burning.

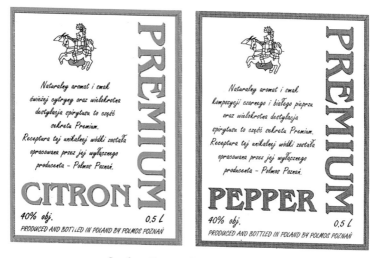

Starka. Rye vodka made to a 16th-century recipe using unrectified rye spirit (originally one of the *gorzalka* style of vodkas) and in accordance with the traditional recipe a little Malaga wine is added, before spending at least 10 years in small oak casks. Vanilla, cream nose, with a rich, tannic quality and characteristic rye flavour. 50 per cent.

Tatra. Originally produced in the Tatra mountains of southern Poland. Based on angelica, it has a flavour of herbs and spices with angelica dominating. Has a refreshing herbaceousness. 45 per cent.

Tevie. Multiply-distilled kosher grain vodka.

Turowka. Herbal infusions, including bison grass, give this yellow-green vodka a herbaceousness which is considered a good digestif.

U Rebeka. Kosher range produced by Polmos Lancut, spanning clear, orange and plum styles.

Vistula. Potato vodka made from potatoes cultivated along the banks of the Vistula, Poland's key river which flows through Cracow and Warsaw. Smooth with a natural sweetness.

Opposite and above

As the name implies, Premium is exceptionally smooth – as it should be after being distilled four times.

125

Wisniowka. Cherry vodka produced using the juice and infusion of selected Polish cherries especially cultivated for production of Wisniowka. Full, rich but dry flavour.

Wyborowa. Poland's most famous export brand made from twice-rectified rye spirit to a recipe dating from the 16th century, using only specific varieties of rye. The natural, subtle sweetness is definitely the result of the double rectification and refining process, not to added extras. Distinctive retro-chic label designed in 1962, available in two strengths, Blue (40 per cent) and Red (45 per cent). Wyborowa Lemon, Pineapple, Orange, Peach and Pepper are flavoured line extensions. 38 per cent.

POLISH VODKA

LANCUT

WÓDKA
1784

FRANZ JOSEF I
KAISER

PARIS 1900

WYBOROWA

37.5% 100% PURE GRAIN
POLANDS BEST e 70cl

FINEST **VODKA** POLAND

Above
Lancut in south-east Poland is the country's oldest working distillery.
Opposite
Poland's most famous brand.

Zubrowka. While Zubrowka is more easily referred to as Bison Brand, that doesn't mean any part of a bison is used to flavour it. While herds of bison do roam freely in their natural habitat in eastern Poland's Bialowieza National Forest, it is bison grass which provides the flavouring. Technically referred to in Latin as *hierochloe odorata* and *hierochloe australis*, (and in Polish as *zubra trawka*) this wild grass only grows in the Bialowieza Forest. It is picked while in full bloom during the summer, the theory being that the higher the temperature, the better the flavour. Techniques of drying and harvesting the grass, as well as distilling methods, create a highly aromatic flavoured vodka, with a distinctive herby-grassy softness, and a transparent, yellowish green colour.

"It smells of freshly mown hay and spring flowers, of thyme and lavender, and it is so soft on the palate and so comfortable, it is like

Right
The real stuff,
flavoured with
delicious bison grass.

listening to music by moonlight," wrote Somerset Maugham in *The Razor's Edge.*

According to Polish folklore, Zubrowka yields medicinal benefits, not to mention imparting the strength of the bison. Drinking a moderate amount certainly makes one feel better, while any more can at least create the illusion of one having a bison's strength. Extraordinarily smooth, this is a connoisseur's vodka with herbal notes embracing lavender, thyme and even a hint of tobacco. Natural warmth carries through all the way, an extraordinary achievement.

Above

A range of recently introduced kosher vodkas.

DANZKA®
VODKA OF DENMARK
Danish Vodka

Product of Denmark
700 ml 50% alc./vol.
100% grain neutral spirit
Produced and bottled by

Damisco Distillers
1911 Copenhagen Denmark
Danisco A/S

50%vol   70cl

IMPORTED

DANZKA®
VODKA OF DENMARK
Danish Vodka

Product of Denmark
700 ml 40% alc./vol.
100% grain neutral spirit
Produced and bottled by

Damisco Distillers
1911 Copenhagen Denmark
Danisco A/S

40%vol   70cl

IMPORTED

DANZKA®
CITRUS
FLAVOURED VODKA
Citron

Product of Denmark
700 ml 40% alc./vol.
100% grain neutral spirit
Produced and bottled by

Damisco Distillers
Copenhagen Denmark
Danisco A/S

40%vol   70cl

IMPORTED

DANZKA®
BLACKCURRANT
FLAVOURED VODKA
Currant

Product of Denmark
700 ml 40% alc./vol.
100% grain neutral spirit
Produced and bottled by

Damisco Distillers
1911 Copenhagen Denmark
Danisco A/S

40%vol   70cl

IMPORTED

THE REST

AUSTRIA

Piolunowka. A bitters vodka produced by JA Baczewski in Vienna. 29 per cent.

1777 Lviv. A bitters vodka produced by Gessler, using a traditional Ukrainian recipe.

Opposite
Denmark's main entry into the Scandinavian vodka stakes.

BELARUS

Ababycabl. Hailing from Minsk. Grainy flavour, with rye notes giving the smoothness a palatable edge, and gentle burning sensation.

DENMARK

Danzka. Grain vodka distilled in Aalborg, northern Denmark by Danisco Distillers and bottled in an aluminium presentation. Red Label 40 per cent and Blue Label 50 per cent. Danzka Citron and Currant flavoured line extensions.

Fris Vodka Skandia. Produced by a joint venture between Danisco Distillers and Allied Domecq Spirits & Wines.

Hot'n'Sweet. Has a sub-title of "extra hot". Produced by NiWenco APS distillery in Helsingor. 29 per cent.

ENGLAND

Opposite
Smirnoff capitalizes
on its Russian
heritage.
Below are two
clean, grainy vodkas
distilled in Britain
by Greenall's –
Selekt and the
rather macabre
Black Death.

Black Death. Dreamed up by the team at Greenall's who conceived Vladivar qv. Designed as "the vodka in bad taste" with an advertising campaign to match. The vodka is a straightforward spirit, with a grainy feel. 37.5 per cent.

Borzoi. Distilled by James Burrough, part of Allied Domecq. 37.5 per cent.

Cossack. Produced by JJ Vickers, a subsidiary of United Distillers. 37.5 per cent.

Selekt. Standard vodka made by Greenall's, destined for the Russian and duty-free markets. Nevertheless, like all this distillery's products, it is clean and grainy.

Smirnoff: Red label, 37.5 per cent; Silver label, 45.2 per cent and Blue label 45 and 50 per cent. Also a Smirnoff Citrus. (see page 91).

Virgin. A joint venture between Scotch whisky distiller William Grant & Sons and The Virgin Trading Co., forming Virgin Spirits Ltd. Triple-distilled. 37.5, 40 and 50 per cent

Vladivar. Triple-distilled by Whyte & Mackay Imperial. Silver is 40 per cent; Gold is 52 per cent. Also Vladivar Lemon and Peach flavoured line extensions. 37.5 per cent.

SMIRNOFF

THE IMPERIAL RUSSIAN COURT
PIERRE SMIRNOFF
PURVEYORS EST 1818 MOSCOW
1877 · 1886-1917

PRODUCT OF
Ste *Pierre Smirnoff* Fls®
Смирновская Водка №21
REG. U.S. PAT. OFFICE
VODKA
DISTILLED FROM PREMIUM GRAIN
40% ALC. BY VOL. • 80 PROOF

Distilled under the formula and processes of Pierre Smirnoff Sons, successors to world-famed Pierre Smirnoff, Moscow, Russia, Purveyors to the Czars, 1886-1917.
DISTILLED BY STE PIERRE SMIRNOFF FLS®, IN HARTFORD, CT, ALLEN PARK, MI, MENLO PARK, CA

SMIRNOFF

THE IMPERIAL RUSSIAN COURT
PIERRE SMIRNOFF
EST 1818 MOSCOW
1877 · 1886-1917

PRODUCT OF
Ste *Pierre Smirnoff* Fls®
Смирновская Водка №57
REG. U.S. PAT OFFICE
VODKA
DISTILLED FROM PREMIUM GRAIN
50% ALC. BY VOL • 100 PROOF

Distilled under the formula and processes of Pierre Smirnoff Sons, successors to world-famed Pierre Smirnoff, Moscow, Russia, Purveyors to the Czars, 1886-1917.
DISTILLED BY STE PIERRE SMIRNOFF FLS®, IN HARTFORD, CT, ALLEN PARK, MI, MENLO PARK, CA

SELEKT
IMPORTED
СУХАЯ ИМПЕРСКАЯ
VODKA

EST 1761
PRODUCED BY RICHMOND DISTILLERS LTD., WARRINGTON, UNITED KINGDOM

Black Death
VODKA®
GOLD AWARD 1986
GOLD AWARD 1987
Distilled and Bottled under supervision of the
SIGURDSSON FAMILY
Not genuine without my signature
70 cl   Serve Ice Cold   40% alc/vol

Right
Estonia makes its bid for a share of the market with this grain vodka with added sugar.

Opposite
Another Estonian vodka – the rich and creamy Eesti Viin and Koskenkorva, a Finnish favourite.

ESTONIA

Eesti Viin. Grain vodka produced by Liviko Distilleries in Tallinn. Rich, creamy and grainy. 38 per cent.

Viru Valge. Grain vodka with added sugar produced by the Liviko Distilleries, filtered through charcoal.

Monopol. Produced by AS Remedia in Kiiu. 37.5 per cent.

FINLAND

Finlandia. Grain vodka created in 1970 for the export market, particularly the USA. The distinctive bottle featuring a white reindeer stems from Finnish legend. During a winter's night a spell was cast on a young beauty, transforming her into a white reindeer, and naturally endless hunters tried to capture her. The girl's lover was among them, and when he received a fateful wound his blood broke the spell, and she became a young beauty all over again. However, it wasn't exactly a case of living happily ever after as they then fell asleep – permanently.

According to another legend, if you see the sun, moon and a white reindeer at the same time, anything you wish for will come true. Arctic Cranberry and Arctic Pineapple flavoured line extensions launched 1994.

FINLANDIA

VODKA OF FINLAND

Imported

DISTILLED FROM GRAIN

DISTILLED AND BOTTLED BY OY ALKO AB, HELSINKI FINLAND

DISTILLERY ESTABLISHED 1888

50% alc./vol.

Koskenkorva. Introduced in 1952, this grain vodka is one of the most popular on the domestic market. 40, 50 and 60 per cent. Koskenkorva Vargtass (14.5 per cent), Peach (21 per cent) and Pink Cat (21 per cent) are flavoured line extensions.

Leningrad Cowboys. Developed by Primalco in collaboration with the rock band, Leningrad Cowboys. The label features Lenin in sunglasses and with a unicorn rocker's hairstyle. 50 per cent.

Opposite
Even the Russians (grudgingly) admire Finnish vodkas.

FRANCE

Fauchon. From the food and drink emporium in Paris, an own-label Polish grain vodka.

GERMANY

Gorbatschow. In 1921 the Gorbatschow family, former owners of a distillery in St Petersburg, fled to Berlin where they set up shop to distil vodka, initially sold to their fellow-refugees. In 1960 the brand was acquired by another firm which later merged with Henkell, makers of sekt. The brand has since gone on to capture nearly half the German market and is now being widely exported. Gorbatschow, like a number of other brands, attributes its success to the quality of the special filtration process employed. 37.5, 40, 50, and 60 per cent.

Puschkin. Original, and flavoured line extensions Black Sun (wild berries and Siberian roots) and Red (blood oranges) distilled by IB Berentzen.

Rasputin. Grain vodka in two clear styles, Magic (37.5 per cent) and Prestige (40 per cent) within an ice-blue bottle. Produced by Dethleffsen, founded in 1738 and one of Germany's leading spirit producers. A 70 per cent style is also produced. Rasputin Citron and Cranberry are flavoured line extensions.

IRELAND

Hussar. Launched in 1970 by Irish Distillers, triple distilled from grain.

ITALY

Keglevich. Lemon, Peach and Melon styles produced by Stock in Trieste. 30 per cent. Sweet, sticky alcoholic lemonade flavours.

Lemon Vodka. Produced by Villa Colonna. 26 per cent.

Liudka Vodka e Pesca. Peach vodka produced by Averna. 27 per cent.

MONGOLIA

Arkhi. Produced by the Mongolian Vodka Spirit Factory in Ulan Bator, subtitled "The Original Mongolian Vodka" on the label. Quite watery beneath a medicinal flavour. 38 per cent.

NETHERLANDS

Royalty. Produced at the Hooghoudt Distillery, established in 1888 in the northern Dutch town of Groningen, in the region then known as the granary of Holland. Wheat vodka packaged in blue bottles which was the colour of "nobility and dignity" for centuries. Filtered through the active carbon in peat from the north of Holland which the company says has an open structure that exposes a very large surface area to the alcohol. Each bottle bears the seal of the Royal Court of Holland, having been established purveyors to Her Majesty Queen Beatrix in 1988.

Ursus. The Latin word for bear, which is immediately apparent in the Polar bear branding. The recipe for this grain vodka is traditional Icelandic from the beginning of this century, as distilled by a typical bootlegger family (distilling was then illegal in Iceland). Produced by De Hoorn, one of the Netherlands largest distillers. Ursus Lemon and Blackcurrant are flavoured line extensions.

ABSOLUT
Country of Sweden
VODKA

*This superb vodka
was distilled from grain grown
in the rich fields of Southern Sweden.
It has been produced at the famous
old distilleries near Åhus
in accordance with more than
400 years of Swedish tradition.
Vodka has been sold under the name
Absolut since 1879.*

40% VOL.   700 ML.
IMPORTED
PRODUCED AND BOTTLED IN SWEDEN
BY V&S VIN&SPRIT AB.

Left
*Pure spirit or pure
marketing? – Absolut
has become the designer
face of vodka.*

143

SCOTLAND

Grant's. Produced by John Grant in Ayrshire. 37.5 per cent.

Karinskaya. Produced by Campbell's Distillers. 37.5 per cent.

Sergei. Named after the Russian ballet dancer Sergei Lukin, who appears on the label. Available in clear, cherry and spiced flavours.

SLOVENIA

Fructal. Peach vodka cocktail base from Po Ajdovscina. 25 per cent.

SWEDEN

Absolut. Sharp, spirity nose, some grainy warmth that carries to the palate and into the finish. 40 and 50 per cent, Citron, Peppar and Kurant flavours, (see page 88).

UKRAINE

Gorilka. *Gorilka*, meaning burning, was the term for Ukrainian vodka as distinct from Moscow's rye vodkas. Favourite drink of the Cossacks of the lower Dnieper. Made from twice-rectified grain spirit and flavoured with natural linden honey. Nice grainy, oily nose, light on the palate, with good depth. A good mix of concentration and oiliness, quite creamy.

WOLFSCHMIDT

Purveyors to Czars Alexander III and Nicholai II

GENUINE

750ml

Since 1847

VODKA

DISTILLED FROM GRAIN   40% ALC./VOL. (80 PROOF)

Opposite
Another vodka
based on an old
emigré formula.

USA

Smirnoff Silver. Premium version produced by Pierre Smirnoff in Hartford, Connecticut. 45.2 per cent.

Tanqueray Sterling. A line extension to Tanqueray gin and essentially for the USA market. 40 and 50 per cent

Wolfschmidt. The Wolfschmidt family supplied the Russian Tsars Nicholas II and Alexander III from their distillery in Latvia. Possibly the first to import vodka to the USA in early 1900s. Owned by James Beam Distilling.

CHAPTER THREE

SERVING VODKA

V ODKA HAS A COMPREHENSIVE REPERTOIRE,
WHETHER IT IS SERVED NEAT, ON THE ROCKS,
WITH A MIXER OR AS A COCKTAIL. WHILE THERE
ARE PLENTY OF ESTABLISHED COMBINATIONS,
VODKA'S VERSATILITY ALSO PROMOTES INNOVATION.

The authentic way to serve vodka is straight from the freezer, following the Eastern European tradition. While this distinguishes vodka from other spirits, it is by no means the only way it can be served, and Eastern Europeans also serve vodka at room temperature, allowing its aroma and flavours to blossom (and there are plenty of complex vodkas that benefit from this).

On the other hand, chilling vodka heightens the predominant flavour at the expense of other nuances, while also reducing any "burn". Chilling anonymous vodka is always beneficial – though the most it can do is to provide an effect rather than flavour. Vodka glasses should also come out of the freezer (for the truly

Opposite
The classic
Vodkatini – note
the olive. When
replaced by a pearl
onion the drink is
called a Gibson.

chilled experience), as an unchilled glass soon raises the temperature of its contents. Glasses are usually small enough to hold about 50ml, which is a sensible measure, and visually the vodka shouldn't appear lost in a large glass.

Shooting vodka (the modern term for drinking it down-in-one) is another Eastern European cliché. Again, this is only half right, as there are no rules about how vodka should be drunk. While there's never a shortage of sharp shooters (and during a session a typical Polish refrain is *do dna* – to the bottom of the glass), vodka is just as often sipped, with no loss of machismo. It all depends on where your priorities lie: the effect of the alcohol, or enjoying the flavour. If the vodka is anonymous then there's nothing to be gained in lingering, and shooting vodka certainly entails greater theatricality. Aficionados also claim that if the vodka has been chilled the resulting sensation is more intense.

The customary Russian and Polish toast, *na zdrowie* – your health – is more than just a social nicety as vodka is renowned for having a lower level of congeners (impurities which cause hangovers) than many other spirits. This also depends on the amount consumed.

The ritual of shooting vodka is also acquiring optional extras. The "lemon drops" routine, for instance, involves biting a slice of lemon dipped in sugar immediately after downing the shot of vodka.

Opposite
"Leaves you breathless" – the original version of the famous Smirnoff line. Heublein first marketed Smirnoff in America as *"white whiskey".*

Opposite
When drinkers
needed to open a
can of orange juice
to mix with vodka,
they naturally used
a screwdriver.

Temperature is an important factor with flavoured styles. *Krupnik*, for instance, with its complement of wild honey and spices, is often gently heated, which helps to release its complex structure.

MIXERS

The appeal of using vodka with mixers is limited if you really want to appreciate its presence, but virtually unlimited if you are merely looking for a means of adding alcohol to the mixer. Drinking vodka on the rocks is the simplest form of adding a mixer, the water from the melting ice diluting the vodka. This used to be frowned upon, but as fashion is cyclical, a little dilution is now considered "in", and can only benefit anonymous brands.

Adding soda water, a slice of lime or lemon and even a dash of bitters to vodka on the rocks is another option. And a vodka with character is still discernible in this type of long drink.

Fruit juices are a popular partner for vodka, in particular orange juice (a combination known as the Screwdriver) and grapefruit juice, though both conceal the presence of neutral vodka (and for fans of neutral brands that's the whole point).

According to legend, adding orange juice to vodka dates from the USA's Prohibition era, when the raw flavour of bootleg spirit needed to be tempered. Orange juice was the answer, although at that time it was canned, and did

THE POINT OF A SCREWDRIVER IS SMIRNOFF Orange juice is delicious. Smirnoff keeps it that way. That's the whole point of using Smirnoff Vodka. Because smooth, flawless Smirnoff has no taste, it never clashes with the flavor of fruit juice or soft drinks. To make a Smirnoff Screwdriver, just pour a jigger of Smirnoff over ice cubes, fill glass with orange juice and stir. If you've never tried one, you should. *It's America's favorite vodka drink!*

it leaves you breathless ***Smirnoff***®

THE WORLD'S LARGEST SELLING VODKA

Opposite
Russchian, the
successful mixer
made by the
company that made
its fortune from
G (and V) & T.

not have a great taste, so that sugar was added to improve it. Following the repeal of Prohibition, this approach was applied to vodka which is why traditional Screwdriver recipes include sugar. The drink owes its name to the fact that the bootleggers opened cans of orange juice by piercing them with a screwdriver.

A more recent combination, gaining cult status in Poland and Japan, is Zubrowka with apple juice, which still allows the vodka's complex flavours to surface. Cranberry juice is also vodka-friendly, as the flavours remain at the front of the palate, leaving room for the vodka to emerge.

Despite the popularity of vodka and tonic, there is no disguising the fact that vodka is being used here as a gin-substitute. However, the V and T is a completely different drink from the G and T. Gin's botanicals generally retain a greater presence after tonic has been added, whereas many of vodka's are masked by the tonic's quinine content.

Vodka and cola is another form of substitution, this time for rum, or rather Bacardi. Cola also annihilates vodka flavours, so the motivation is the flavour of the cola. The same applies to ginger ale.

In contrast to other spirits, vodka enjoys the distinction of having a mixer devised especially for it in the form of Russchian, launched in the late 1970s by Schweppes. The rise in vodka consumption, coupled with the absence of a

widely accepted mixer, provided a clear market opportunity. In the quest for an original mixer for vodka, but one which was also a pleasant straight drink, Schweppes originally assessed more than 100 flavours. These were shortlisted to four before production began. And who could resist such advertising slogans as "Order your vodka in Russchian"? Russchian did, however, also succeed as a straight drink without vodka, which speaks volumes for its flavour. It certainly would not be impaired by neutral vodka, though how much it adds to a quality brand is a matter of personal opinion.

COCKTAILS

Opposite

Two shakes –
vodka came in to its
own as a mixer
during the cocktail
era and is currently
going through
something of a
renaissance.

Cocktails pose the same question as mixers: are they an effective medium for vodka, or just a case of interesting flavour combinations merely fortified by alcohol? While vodka claims its own authentic (as well as substitute) cocktails, the range is so broad that it can support either point of view.

Nevertheless, cocktails are back in fashion, with the kitsch umbrella-and-sparklers style of the 1980s being replaced by more sophisticated presentations and flavours. Moreover, the current cocktail-ization of the USA has largely been generated by vodka. Indeed, a new generation of vodka cocktails uses the term "Martini" as a generic reference. A French Martini means vodka, Chambord liqueur and pineapple juice, while a Polish Martini results from a combination of Krupnik, Wyborowa and apple juice.

This contemporary movement has not, however, overshadowed the original Dry Martini cocktail, which retains more mystique, and devotees, than any other cocktail in living memory (and consequently an above-average number of Martini bores). The Dry Martini was apparently invented around 1910 by a bartender, Signor Martini, working in New York's Knickerbocker Hotel. In the meantime, all sorts of nonsense has been added to the Dry Martini myth, such as the vermouth content being only a shaft of light passing through the

VODKA TONIC

BLOODY MARY

BLACK RUSSIAN

MOSCOW MULE

SCREWDRIVER

VODKA MARTINI

bottle of vermouth into the glass, or turning reverentially in the direction of France or Italy while shaking it.

The origins of Vodka Martini, also known under the amalgamated reference Vodkatini, were merely as a change from gin. But the success of the Vodka Martini has been such that vodka has long forgotten it was not Martini's first choice.

The classic English summer drink, Pimm's, was invented in the late 19th century at Pimm's restaurant in the City of London. Originally based on gin and a secret garnish of herbs, the vodka-based version which followed generally does a better job. Vodka underlines the flavours of accessories such as orange, lemon, cucumber and lemonade, whereas gin's botanicals tend to compete, resulting in less focused flavours.

Similarly, gin was originally at the heart of a Bloody Mary. Renowned as a hangover cure, the Bloody Mary is equally good at inflicting one. Its classic match of vodka and tomato juice has a far better rapport than gin, as juniper and tomato juice do not harmonize in the same way.

In addition to the usual extras like lemon juice, Worcester sauce, Tabasco and celery salt, a variable cast of seasoning includes cayenne, horseradish and even sherry (with a stick of celery this can be a meal in itself). But those are just the trimmings. Using different flavoured vodkas such as chilli or pepper makes a

Opposite
This old Smirnoff advertisement encouraged drinkers to experiment with vodka's versatile neutrality.

HARPO MARX, NOTED COMIC AND MUSICIAN, AUTHORS A NEW BEST-SELLER "HARPO SPEAKS." AT BOOK STORES.

WHEN I HONK FOR VODKA, I EXPECT SMIRNOFF Harpo, the silent one, may be excused from naming his brand. But you, gentle reader, should be specific. For, ever since Smirnoff changed the drinking habits of America, countless Johnny-come-lately vodkas have gotten into the act. To assure yourself of the flawless original, always call for your Smirnoff by name. It makes the driest Martinis, the smoothest Screwdrivers, the most delicious drinks of every kind. So know what you drink—drink what you know!

it leaves you breathless

Smirnoff
THE GREATEST NAME IN **VODKA**

80 AND 100 PROOF. DISTILLED FROM GRAIN. © STE. PIERRE SMIRNOFF FLS. (DIVISION OF HEUBLEIN), HARTFORD, CONN., 1961

significant difference. Meanwhile, freshly squeezed tomato juice yields a lighter result than the tinned version, whereas "clamato" is an irresistible combination of clam juice and tomato juice. When serving a Bloody Mary, professionals recommend using no more than three lumps of ice.

The more subtle Bullshot, with beef (or game) consommé, Worcester sauce, lemon juice and pepper, is more suitable to highlight vodka, while the Bloodshot combines the merits of both cocktails.

Vodka cocktails have not always had to trail gin. In fact, plenty of cocktails have been invented specifically to honour vodka. Moscow Mule is hailed as the original vodka cocktail, now being revived. Its origins lie in 1940s Hollywood; venue – the Cock and Bull Bar (perhaps an apt term for the Moscow Mule legend). Apparently there copper mugs were made up with the names of movie stars, and in them a combination of vodka, lime juice and ginger beer was served. (Now missing, these mugs are a Holy Grail for bartenders.) Another possible explanation is that the bar had a vast stock of ginger beer, and the cocktail was devised merely as a way to get rid of it. Then again, what begins as a practical measure can still be promoted as a speciality.

Liqueurs also combine readily with vodka in cocktails such as Black Russian, made with the addition of Kahlua, and White Russian, in

Opposite
Smirnoff leaves Harpo Marx speechless as well as breathless. During the 1960s Heublein used a cocktail of familiar faces to promote their vodka – everyone from Benny Goodman to Zsa Zsa Gabor.

which Cacao and cream are added. And it only takes a measure of Galliano to change a long drink (Screwdriver) into the Harvey Wallbanger cocktail. The eponymous Harvey was a Californian surfer who (allegedly) spent endless evenings drinking endless Screwdrivers, to which he added a dash of Galliano. That meant it always took more than one attempt for him to locate the door when leaving the bar, and his banging into the walls in the process yielded the name for the cocktail.

FLAVOURING VODKA

Flavoured vodkas have been popular ever since the 19th century when over 100 different flavours were produced. Today, DIY flavouring is becoming more widespread, yielding good results on the straightforward basis of macerating fruit, herbs and spices, or by combining favourites such as orange segments and couverture (the best quality chocolate, containing the highest percentage of cocoa).

One of the quickest flavouring options is to use a vanilla pod or a potent herb such as tarragon, which would be fully infused in about four days, using vodka at 40 per cent abv. Similarly, chilli peppers need about a week, while flavourings such as lemon zest generally require a month. For a caramel style, sugar syrup can be added to vodka before it begins to set. The proportion of flavourings used, and when the vodka is "ready", are obviously a

Left
Aiming – wittily –
for the Bloody Mary
market with a
pepper vodka.

matter of personal preference, so tastings should be conducted en route. If necessary, Polish Pure Spirit can be added to bring the resulting vodka "up to strength", or it may be used for the maceration process, particularly for soft fruit such as raspberries, using just enough spirit to cover the fruit, then reducing the strength to a palatable level by adding regular strength vodka.

Fruits such as sour cherries and plums usually work best if they are prepared beforehand by bringing them to the boil with sugar to help release the flavours.

CHAPTER FOUR

VODKA WITH FOOD

V ODKA'S INTEGRAL ROLE IN BOTH RUSSIAN AND POLISH LIFE HAS RESULTED IN BOTH COUNTRIES DEVELOPING A GASTRONOMIC CULTURE OF DRINKING VODKA WITH FOOD. THIS HAS LED TO THE DEVELOPMENT OF A SERIES OF SNACK FOODS.

Not just any old snack, but a specific range of hors d'oeuvres, referred to as *zakuski* in Russian and *zakaski* in Polish. It is not just the names that are similar, as many of the same dishes are served by both countries, and include specialities like caviar and smoked sturgeon (though vodka combines equally well with humbler items like salt herring, pickled mushrooms, dill cucumbers and charcuterie).

Zakuski reflect the traditions of preserving that shaped Polish and Russian cuisine – pickling, smoking, salting and drying – all of which produce robust and intense flavours that vodka can balance.

These culinary traditions also provide the essential accessories for *zakuski*, such as soured cream and curd cheese. More "subliminal" links between vodka and *zakuski* are a duplication of

Opposite
Yes, the best caviar does go with the best vodka.

163

raw ingredients: rye in bread as well as Extra Zytnia and Wyborowa; wheat in *blinis* (pancakes), echoed in Sibirskaya.

Although salty, spicy flavours are a common denominator of *zakuski*, encouraging further consumption of vodka quite naturally, there is also a genuine relationship between the vodka and the food, as the flavours harmonize and enhance each other on the palate.

As well as performing a balancing act, vodka also promotes the flavours of charcuterie, particularly sausage, as well as the pronounced flavours of dill cucumbers, pickled mushrooms and favourite condiments such as mustard.

While caviar (sturgeon roe) is the most celebrated partner for vodka, it is not simply a case of combining two of Russia's finest assets. In fact, vodkas such as Stolichnaya, Cristal and Smirnoff Black make caviar even more of an indulgence. Vodka with beluga caviar promotes a creamy, nutty flavour, together with a hint of sweetness recalling almonds and marzipan. Oscietra's lightly fishy, brie/roquefort taste becomes even smoother with vodka. Similarly, the sea-salt flavour of sevruga is softened, producing a lingering creaminess.

Caviar and vodka combine perfectly with the Russian speciality, *blinis*. Having also been adopted by Finland and Poland, *blinis* provide a natural pedestal for caviar, not to mention other parts of the sturgeon and even other fish, such as herrings and salmon.

Smoked salmon is balanced by a grain vodka such as Finlandia and Absolut, while the natural sweetness of Wyborowa echoes that of the salmon. When salmon is also accompanied by *mizeria* (a Polish salad of thinly sliced cucumber in a sour cream and dill dressing), Belweder allows the flavours to surface after some initial "central heating". Typical accompaniments for smoked fish, such as pickled gherkins and dill cucumbers, are emphasized by rye and other grain vodkas such as Finlandia.

Gravadlax (raw salmon marinated in salt and dill) served with dill mustard and rye bread, is a Swedish speciality that has become an international success, and a glass of Absolut is its native partner. Other Scandinavian specialities that traditionally accompany vodka are crayfish and salted roe, which are tailor-made for locals such as Finlandia.

Herrings are a staple in Poland, Russia and Scandinavia, and various methods of preparing them have evolved, whether smoked, soused in vinegar, fried, chopped, or salted. Salt herring fillets are typically accompanied by rye bread, garnished with chopped onion, or apple slices and horseradish sauce, though the most popular dressing is soured cream, with or without mustard. Either way, grain vodka melts the richness of the cream and slices through the oiliness of the herring, while a flavoured vodka such as Zubrowka puts the accent on the mustard (particularly if grain mustard is used).

Herrings are also frequently served with potatoes in Russia and Poland, ideally with a prime grain vodka. But there is also a natural link with the creamy flavour of potato vodka (providing a portion each of distilled and boiled potatoes).

A potato vodka like Luksusowa embraces the rustic version of *blinis*: grated potato pancakes with various toppings, such as smoked salmon or herrings and soured cream. An even simpler base is rye bread, with Absolut Pepper or Pertsovka perking up a topping of smoked salmon, soured cream and caviar. Wisniowka is a good partner for rye bread, following a bread-and-cherry-jam principle, with rye bread also emphasizing the tomato flavours and seasoning of a Bloody Mary cocktail.

Curd cheese is used in a variety of Russian and Polish dishes, such as patties which combine the cheese with mashed potatoes, flour and eggs, before being fried and served with soured cream. A typical Polish favourite are *leniwe pierogi*, literally lazy *pierogi* (because a simpler *pierogi* enclose a separate filling, while in *leniwe* the filling – usually curd cheese – is mixed directly into the dough). Once boiled, *leniwe* are garnished with bacon lardons or fried onion. Extra Zytnia provides an earthy base for the cheese and dough flavours, while Zubrowka highlights the curd and bacon.

DURING THE MEAL

Not surprisingly, people from countries where there is no established vodka tradition have a mental block about drinking vodka during a meal, and the thought of a spirit that's usually 40 per cent abv probably suggests alcoholic excess – though it's obviously not drunk in the same quantities as wine. And yet, a measure of vodka has the same alcoholic content as a glass of wine. Moreover, when it comes to matching vodka with food, *zakuski* provide a variety of flavours that work well with vodka, and flavour combinations are, after all, what it's all about.

While *zakuski* play a supporting role to vodka, it is more usual for vodka to be tailored to the food during a meal. This imposes no restrictions, because just like wine, vodka spans a wide range of styles: from sweet to dry, from herbaceous and spicy to fruity.

Just as the origins of vodka are disputed by the Poles and Russians, so both countries claim the credit for devising their national dish, *pirozhki* in Russian (dating from the 12th century, *pir* meaning feast) and *pierogi* in Polish. For ease of reference to Westerners, this dish is described as a type of ravioli, but that makes them sound derivative rather than a speciality in their own right. While the dough is made from plain flour and eggs, like pasta, *pierogi* are infinitely superior, at least in terms of size, and consequently in the amount of filling. Curd cheese blended with mashed potato and onion is the standard filling, followed by mushrooms mixed with either meat or cabbage/sauerkraut. Ground beef combined with onions and breadcrumbs is another option, and buckwheat is the traditional filling. Regional variations also include brains. A Russian and Polish variation is to use various types of pastry, such as yeast or puff pastry, instead of dough. *Pierogi* are served à la Polonaise (a garnish of fried breadcrumbs in melted butter), or with a soured cream sauce. Such a combination needs full-flavoured grain vodka such as Gorilka, Stolichnaya or Extra Zytnia.

The Russian love of pies is behind the ever-popular *kulebiak*, and then there is the Finnish equivalent *lohitiiras*, featuring salmon, hard-boiled eggs and rice. Vodka's affinity with salmon, plus its ability to melt pastry, makes a brand such as Stolovaya or Finlandia an essential partner.

Carp in grey sauce actually refers to a gingerbread sauce. Surprisingly, this historic Polish dish is not overpowered by Extra Zytnia, which focuses the ginger flavours and promotes a long aftertaste of carp, while Pieprzowka balances the sauce with the carp.

Polish hunters traditionally take a flask of Zubrowka out with them, and this vodka, as well as Wyborowa and Extra Zytnia, is a typical accompaniment to *bigos* (hunter's stew). *Bigos* was originally made with whatever the hunter managed to bag, possibly duck or venison. The usual additions include onions, fresh cabbage or sauerkraut (or a combination of both), sausage, sour apples, prunes, tomatoes, mushrooms and juniper berries.

Another variation on the cabbage theme are *golubtsi* in Russian and *golabki* (literally little pigeons) in Polish. The dish consists of cabbage leaves stuffed with rice, minced pork or veal, and mushrooms, while the most traditional filling is buckwheat. The robust flavours (particularly that of the cabbage) strike a chord with full-bodied vodkas, such as Gorilka and Extra Zytnia. Flavoured vodkas are also a good choice. Zubrowka announces itself clearly before allowing the ingredients to have their say, while Pertsovka highlights the seasoning and "nuttiness" of the rice.

The rich flavours of beef Stroganoff are effortlessly balanced by vodkas such as Stolichnaya, Stolovaya and Gorilka. Now an icon of haute cuisine, this dish is thought to have been developed for the 19th-century Russian diplomat Count Stroganoff by his French chef. However, various prototypes for this recipe were known in Russia from the 18th century.

Zrazy (beef roulades) were well established in the Polish repertoire by the 14th century when they gained a royal pedigree, being a favourite of King Ladislaus. Beef sirloin is beaten and rolled around a filling of bacon or smoked ham, chopped dill cucumber and grain mustard. After being sealed in a frying pan, *zrazy* are casseroled, and usually served with buckwheat or pearl barley. Zubrowka really perks up the dill cucumber and mustard grains, and the latter are also underlined by Jarzebiak. Potato and nut dumplings with cinnamon and soured cream are a classic Russian dessert and can be uplifted by cherry vodka. The lingering aftertaste of pure cherry makes it seem as though the dumplings de-alcoholized the vodka. A superior grain style like Gorilka also works wonders, combining perfectly with the nuts as well as lightening the cream.

Another Russian and Polish favourite is pancakes filled with cream or curd cheese. These are lightened by flavoured vodkas such as Goldwasser and Starka, and these "dessert" styles also continue beautifully as a digestif.

AROUND THE WORLD

Vodka combines so well with Polish, Russian and Scandinavian dishes that its rapport with other international cuisines is frequently overlooked. However diverse the menu, the same principles apply.

This means that cream, however it is served, always benefits from vodka. A prime example is soup: watercress soup with soured cream becomes lighter and more animated when accompanied by a vodka such as Smirnoff Black or Stolichnaya. Similarly, the rich flavours of a traditional fish soup with croutons and *aioli* (garlic mayonnaise), or *rouille* (garlic and pepper sauce), become even smoother with vodka.

A Gorgonzola tart, providing the extra challenge of rich cheese, is easily dealt with by Smirnoff Black. Other rich, robust dishes such as seabass, fishcakes, fillet of beef, and veal chop with mashed potatoes, are balanced by vodkas like Wyborowa or Gorilka. And why reach for Sauternes when foie gras melts into a luxurious mouthful when accompanied by a pedigree grain vodka.

Rich flavours can also be a characteristic of "light" dishes, such as Caesar Salad with its garlic and Parmesan dressing, garlic croutons and anchovies. Here, a vodka such as Smirnoff Black cuts through the croutons and melts the Parmesan in a spectacular manner.

Mediterranean favourites combine well with vodka. Goat's cheese in filo parcels has the sharp flavour of the cheese tempered and made creamier by Stolichnaya. A full-bodied grain vodka makes pumpkin tortellini smoother on the palate, and also underlines the pumpkin flavour. Grilled food is a natural for vodka which promotes the smokey, charred flavours of a dish such as grilled squid.

And there is no need to remind you that rich, creamy desserts, particularly pastry-based, benefit from "dessert" style vodkas such as Starka, Wisniowka, Goldwasser or Krupnik.

CHAPTER FIVE

COOKING
WITH
VODKA

JUST AS VODKA CAN BE AN IDEAL ACCOMPANIMENT
TO FOOD, IT CAN BE EQUALLY EFFECTIVE AS A
FLAVOURING IN VARIOUS SWEET OR SAVOURY DISHES.
VODKA'S ALCOHOLIC CONTENT AND 'BODY' ALSO
ENSURE IT IS A VALUABLE CULINARY ASSET.

But using it as a cooking ingredient does not mean you can get away with a poor quality brand. Cooking only eliminates the alcohol content; it does not improve the flavour of the vodka, so you only get back what you put in.

The general principle of cooking with wines and spirits is to boil off all the alcohol. However, retaining some alcohol (by adding alcohol at the beginning of the cooking process, and topping up at the last minute) is also an advantage, as alcohol contributes a significant amount of flavour and body.

As all alcoholic drinks can be used as flavourings in cooking, many countries have their own traditions of cooking with alcohol

Opposite
Smoked salmon
nicoise is a classic
accompaniment
to vodka.

which means there are many international roles for vodka to step into. Rice wine, for instance, stipulated in various Asian dishes, can be replaced with vodka. The same applies to rum in Caribbean and brandy in French cuisine, particularly for a flambé.

Vodka can also feature in "teetotal" specialities like pesto sauce, where clear grain vodka joins the usual list of ingredients. *Gravadlax* with scrambled eggs is enriched by stirring a vodka/cream mix into the eggs at the last minute, to retain some alcohol.

The link between vodka and tomatoes, created by the Bloody Mary cocktail, has resulted in the cocktail ingredients being served up in alternative ways, such as chilled soup, sorbet, or even a salad dressing. Vodka can also be added to other vinaigrette-style dressings, by using lemon-flavoured vodka instead of fresh lemon juice.

The same principles apply when using vodka as a marinade. Clear vodka combined with olive oil and lime juice is suited to a ceviche of scallops, while Limonnaya or Pertsovka can be used with fish such as salmon, or even poultry and meat. Zubrowka is an effective marinade for earthy specialities like boar, adding flavour as well as tenderizing the meat over several days. Other meats such as pork and beef need far less time to benefit.

The marinade also provides the basis for a cooking liquor, and consequently a sauce: only needing to be reduced and flavoured with the likes of mushrooms, herbs, stock and cream.

Deglazing is another method of creating an instant sauce: add vodka to the pan after sautéeing or roasting meat, raise the heat and blend the vodka with the cooking juices, while scraping any remnants from the surface of the pan. Once the alcohol has boiled off (or not, as you prefer), the finishing touches can be added.

Following the tradition of serving fruit-flavoured sauces with meat, a black cherry vodka sauce really revs up lamb roasted with rosemary and a herb crust. This sauce also harmonizes well with accompaniments such as mashed potatoes and carrot purée. Lamb can also be marinated in cherry vodka, then cooked with morello cherries which have had the same cherry vodka treatment.

Pertsovka or Absolut Pepper are an effective addition to spicy, Asian style sauces, whereas the herbaceous flavour of Zubrowka is particularly good with mushroom, dill and other herb sauces.

A flambé not only looks spectacular, but the flames help brown the food, as well as caramelizing any sugar content. Vodka should be pre-heated for a flambé (below boiling point), and lit before being poured over the dish (cold vodka can be absorbed by food, which defeats the object), while the flames simply extinguish themselves once the alcohol has expired.

BAKING

Baking is another area that benefits from vodka. It is well known that bread contains alcohol, so why not add some alcohol that is actually worth tasting? This is easily done by adding vodka to water, which is worked into the dough. And as vodka combines so well with other favourite ingredients, you can make the most of it by adding, say, sun-dried tomatoes and Parmesan.

In cake- and pastry-making, the end result is lightened by the addition of vodka, especially Polish Pure Spirit. *Faworki,* also known as *chrusty* (delicate pastry twists, several inches long and dredged in icing sugar), are meltingly light despite being deep-fried, and benefit from a dash of vodka. Similarly, preparing doughnuts Warsaw style means adding clear vodka to a rich list of ingredients including yeast, cream, and eggs. Meanwhile, incorporating saffron into the Polish yeast cake, *babka*, is through an infusion using clear grain vodka, which is added to other flavourings like vanilla, almonds and raisins.

DESSERTS

Vodka is on hand to help with dessert: simply sprinkle flavoured vodkas over ready-to-serve fruit, or allow a more leisurely maceration. Finlandia and Polish Pure Spirit in particular, underline the flavour of various berries and soft fruit such as cherries, raspberries and blueberries, which can be prepared as a compote to fill pancakes, along with a dash of soured cream. To flambé a dessert such as crepe suzette, why not use Starka or Soplica, particularly as the residual flavour is mellower than brandy?

Why not add vodka to a *sabayon?* Cherry, strawberry or Absolut Currant vodka are good choices, especially if the *sabayon* is poured over a layer of corresponding fruit (which can also be marinaded in vodka).

Vodka provides a concentrated flavour within a small amount of liquid which makes it an ideal flavouring for ice cream and sorbets. It also improves the texture: since alcohol has a lower freezing point than water, it helps to prevent the formation of sugar crystals and achieve a smoother result. (Adding egg whites is a traditional means of improving texture, but it also diminishes flavours in the process.) Too much vodka, on the other hand, is not the answer as it inhibits the freezing process.

A royal precedent for using Absolut Currant vodka was set by the king and queen of Sweden. They served *Le sorbet de Absolut Kurant* as a palate cleanser (after *Le turbot à la nage au basilic*, and before *Le filet d'agneau aux fleurs de courgette, pommes nouvelles*), at a dinner given for the Norwegian royal couple in 1993 at Drottningholm Castle outside Stockholm.

If you don't actually put any vodka in the sorbet or ice cream, you might pour over it a flavoured style like cherry, lemon or honey for an instant bonus.

RECIPES

TURBOT WITH MASHED POTATOES AND VODKA SAUCE

225g/8oz potatoes, peeled
Milk
Butter
1-2 cloves garlic, crushed
Sprig of thyme
Zest and juice of 1 lemon
1 bulb of fennel
900g/2lb turbot or brill,
  filleted and skinned
Fish stock
50 ml/2 floz clear grain
  vodka
50g/2oz unsalted butter,
  chilled and diced
Salt and pepper
Parsley and chives, chopped

Boil and mash potatoes with milk, butter, garlic, thyme, lemon juice and zest. Meanwhile, slice fennel into 6 pieces and put in a heavy pan (with a tight fitting lid), place fish on top of fennel and season. Add fish stock to barely cover the fish, bring to a simmer and poach for approximately 5 minutes or until cooked. Divide potatoes between two warmed plates, arrange fennel and fish on top. Reduce the cooking liquid by half, whisk in the vodka and butter, add parsley and chives, pour over fish and serve.
Serves 2.

BRUNO LOUBET'S ABSOLUT PEPPER TOMATO CONSOMMÉ

Chop tomatoes into small pieces and place in a liquidizer with remaining ingredients, except the mint. Liquidize for 5 minutes until smooth. Place a muslin cloth in a colander over a glass bowl. Pour the tomato mixture over the cloth and tie the ends of the cloth with string. Put a small plate over the cloth, and weigh down with a heavy weight. Put in the fridge for 3 hours until the mixture is clear. Serve in iced bowl with crushed mint leaves to garnish.
Serves 4.

800g/1 3/4lb ripe tomatoes
1 small garlic clove
Basil leaves
1 red chilli pepper
Salt and pepper
Absolut Pepper vodka,
  to taste
Mint leaves

ALISTAIR LITTLE'S ABSOLUT BLOODY MARY SALAD

For the Bloody Mary sauce:

Celery salt, to taste

1 x 500g/20oz tin tomato
    pieces

1 teaspoon Worcestershire sauce

Double measure Absolut
    Lemon vodka

Double measure Absolut
    Pepper vodka

1/4 teaspoon Tabasco sauce

For the salad:

1 red onion, peeled and diced

1 cucumber, cut into strips,
    cored and sliced into pieces

1 large carrot, peeled and
    diced into small pieces

1 red bell pepper, deseeded
    and diced

1 large stick celery, destrung
    and diced

1 handful coarsely chopped
    Continental parsley leaves

2 tablespoons olive oil

2 tablespoons red wine

Salt and pepper

For the breadcrumbs:

One baguette

Olive oil

To prepare the sauce place all ingredients in a large bowl and refrigerate for at least an hour. Mix all the vegetables in a large bowl and season, then refrigerate until required. Chill soup plates. To prepare the breadcrumbs preheat the oven to 200° C/400°F. Slice the loaf into crouton-like rounds. Brush lightly with olive oil and spread on a baking tray. Toast in oven until golden then bash up in a food processor. Put aside until required. To assemble, mix salad with breadcrumbs, and place a mound in the centre of each cold soup plate. Stir the sauce mix and ladle around the moulded salad.

POTATO, DATE AND APPLE DUMPLINGS

Soak dates/prunes in vodka for at least 30 minutes (the longer you leave them the more alcohol will be absorbed), then place with any remaining vodka in a pan, bring to the boil then drain and mix with orange and lemon zest, juices, chopped nuts and 50g/2oz of the caster sugar. In a large bowl beat the potatoes with most of the flour, together with the lard, egg yolk and salt, working the mixture into a dough. Place some flour on a work surface and knead, adding a little flour if necessary to obtain a smooth, glossy dough. Roll out mixture into 5cm/2in squares. Place a teaspoon of the apple and the prune puree in the middle. Pull the corners up to enclose the filling and shape gently into a ball. Place dumplings in boiling salted water and poach for about 25 minutes, until they float to the top. Drain thoroughly. Combine the cinnamon, breadcrumbs and sugar, then roll the warm dumplings in this mixture. Serve with vanilla ice cream or whipped cream. Serves 4.

15 ready to eat, stoned dates or prunes, chopped
100ml/4floz clear grain vodka
1/4 teaspoon each of grated orange and lemon zest
1 teaspoon each of lemon juice and orange juice
50g/2oz chopped pecan nuts
150g/6oz caster sugar
2 large cooking apples (peeled, cored and cooked to puree with 25g/1oz caster sugar and 2 teaspoons lemon juice, passed through a sieve and cooled)
800g/1 3/4lb mashed potatoes, cooled
250g/8oz plain flour
75g/3oz lard
1 egg yolk
Pinch salt
1/4 teaspoon cinnamon
50g/2oz fresh breadcrumbs, toasted

SCRAMBLED EGGS WITH VODKA AND SMOKED SALMON

8 eggs
2 tablespoons butter
1 tablespoon soured cream
1 tablespoon premium grain
  vodka, or to taste
Smoked salmon
Salt and pepper

Beat eggs in a bowl. Melt butter in a heavy bottomed saucepan on a low heat and add the eggs. Cook slowly, which will make it even creamier, stirring with a wooden spoon. Stir the vodka in to the cream and add this mixture to the eggs once they have reached a creamy consistency and are almost ready. Serve immediately with smoked salmon.
Serves 4.

PASTA WITH VODKA PESTO

Prepare the pesto by pounding the garlic, basil leaves, pine kernels and a little salt in a pestle and mortar. Slowly pour in the olive oil as you keep pounding, then add the cheeses and vodka to form a paste. Cook pasta in salted water until al dente, drain, and toss with the sauce in a heated serving bowl. Serve immediately.
Serves 4.

2 garlic cloves, crushed
2 large bunches fresh basil leaves, torn
1 tablespoon pine kernels
2 tablespoons Parmesan cheese, grated
2 tablespoons Pecorino cheese, grated
100ml/4floz olive oil
Clear grain vodka, to taste
Salt
400g/14oz pasta such as tagliatelle or linguine

INDEX

ACKNOWLEDGEMENTS

The writing of this book was greatly helped by many people. In Poland by Urszula Ludwiczynska, Wanda Moscicka and Lidia Kulesza at Aros in Warsaw and by Elzieta Goldyka, Stanislaw Palonka and Janusz Kujawinski at Polmos. Thanks also to Aleksandra Matuszak, Maciej Kurzawinski and Dariusz Matuszak for help in research in Poland. In Britain our thanks must go to Ruth Jacobs and the staff of the Tsar's Bar at the Langham Hilton, David Steward, Nancy Brady, Liz Hole at W.G. White, Naomi Proudlove and Kamy Sheikh, while Lorna Wing, Lindsay Stewart, Carolyn Cavele, Jan Woroniecki of the Wodka Restuarant, London and the staff at Maze Restaurant, London provided us with recipes as well as food for thought.

RECIPE ACKNOWLEDGEMENTS

Thanks to Bruno Loubet and Alastair Little whose recipes were part of The Absolut Challenge recipe competition sponsored by Absolut vodka; Mark Holmes, head chef at Scotts Restaurant, London and Anthony Marshall, executive chef at the Langham Hilton, London.

PHOTOGRAPHIC CREDITS

Absolut 13, 79, 81, 89, 143, 161; Agros, Poland 22; Alko Exports, Finland 84; Barkers, Scotland 173; Bielsko-Biala Distillery, Poland 14, 16, 65; Galerie Moderne, London 154; James Duncan 146; Henschell & Sohnlein 87; Hulton Getty Picture Collection Limited 30/31, 43; Lancut Museum, Poland 25, 54, 71; Mary Evans Picture Library 6, 7, 39, 44; Marblehead UK 18; Polish Cultural Institute, London 69; Russia & Republics Photolibrary 40; Smirnoff 70, 92, 95, 148, 151, 156, 158; Tarac Australia 69; The Mansell Collection 39, 50; W.G.White, London 162; Zielona Gora Distillery, Poland 29, 66/67